THE MALONE SOCIETY REPRINTS

NO. 72

A LOOKING-GLASS FOR LONDON AND ENGLAND BY THOMAS LODGE & ROBERT GREENE

AMS PRESS

NEW YORK

Library of Congress Cataloging-in-Publication Data

Lodge, Thomas, 1558?–1625.
  A looking-glass for London and England.

  Reprint. Previously published: London: Printed for
the Malone Society by J. Johnson at the Oxford
University Press, 1932. (The Malone Society reprints;
no. 72). Originally published: 1594.
  I. Greene, Robert, 1558?–1592. II. Title.
III. Series: Malone Society reprints; no. 72.
PR2659.L6L5 1985   822'.3   82-45801
ISBN 0-404-63072-3

INTERNATIONAL STANDARD BOOK NUMBER
     SET: 0-404-63000-6
VOLUME: 0-404-63072-3

INTERNATIONAL STANDARD SERIALS NUMBER
0265-4032

AMS PRESS
56 East 13 Street
New York, N.Y. 10003

Except for the addition of the half-title and the copyright entries,
AMS has preserved the collation of the leaves in this reprint.

Reprinted with permission of The Malone Society.

Trim size has been slightly altered. Original trim: 16.8 × 21.7 cm.

MANUFACTURED IN THE UNITED STATES
OF AMERICA

a

PRINTED FOR THE MALONE SOCIETY
BY JOHN JOHNSON AT THE
OXFORD UNIVERSITY
PRESS

A LOOKING-GLASS FOR LONDON AND ENGLAND BY THOMAS LODGE & ROBERT GREENE

1594

THE MALONE SOCIETY
REPRINTS
1932

This reprint of *A Looking-Glass for London and England* has been prepared under the direction of the General Editor.

Dec. 1932.   W. W. Greg.

Printed in Great Britain

The following entries in the books of the Stationers' Company clearly refer to the play here reprinted :

5 [ffebruarij *deleted*] Marcij [1593/4]

Enttred for his copie vnder the wardens, handes / a booke intituled the Tho
lookinge glasse for london / by Tho. lodg. and Robert Greene gent' vj^d Creede
[Register B, fol. 305^a.]

14. Augusti [1600] . . .

Entred for his Copyes by direction of m^r white warden vnder his hand Thomas
wrytinge : These [12] Copyes followinge beinge thinge formerlye printed Pavyer
& sett over to the sayd Thoms Pavyer : viz. . . .
  [10] The lookinge glas for London   vj^d . . .
[Register C, fol. 63^{a,b}.]

In pursuance of the first of these entries Thomas Creede printed an edition which was to be sold by William Barley and bore the date 1594. It is a quarto in black letter (with roman and occasionally italic used incidentally) of a body approximating to modern pica (20 ll. = c. 83 mm.). The only known copy, formerly in the Kemble and Devonshire collections, is now in the Huntington Library, California. It wants the first leaf (A1, presumably blank) while two other leaves (B2, 3) are mutilated. A second edition was printed, again by Creede and to be sold by Barley, with the date 1598. Like the first, which it follows closely, it is a black-letter quarto, and four copies at least have survived. One is in the Garrick collection at the British Museum; two are at the Bodleian Library, one in the Malone collection, and one in the Douce; one is again in the Huntington Library. All four want the first blank leaf, and in the Douce copy four other leaves (A2, 3, I3, 4) are defective. (In the middle of the seventeenth century the Douce copy was in the stock of Thomas Dring, who carried on business as a bookseller from 1649 to 1668, and it bears on the back of the title-leaf a printed label reading : '[Y]ou may be

Furnish'd with most Sorts of Plays, at the White Lion near Chancery-lane end in Fleet-street, by Thomas Dring.') Two years after printing the second edition Creede evidently transferred his rights in the copy to Thomas Pavyer, although his own name does not appear in the entry in the Stationers' Register. In due course a third quarto appeared, printed once more by Creede, but this time for Pavyer as publisher, with the date 1602. It was again set up in black letter and from its immediate predecessor, but not page for page. A copy, apparently the only one known, is at the British Museum, again in the Garrick collection. (It has been mis-dated 1603 on the back.) Another quarto, printed and sold by Bernard Alsop, bears the date 1617. Like the last it was printed from the quarto of 1598, which it followed page for page, but this time in roman type. Alsop had been in partnership with Creede and had lately taken over his stock. Since he went back to the second edition for his copy he may have been ignorant of the rights of Pavyer, who continued in business till 1625. Of this edition there are two copies in the British Museum, one in the Dyce collection at South Kensington, and one (wanting the last leaf) in the Bodleian Library: there is also one in the Huntington Library, one in the Library of Congress, and one in the Boston Public Library: probably others survive. There was yet one other quarto printed, but since the only copy known has lost its title-leaf, it is impossible to say from whose press or exactly when it appeared, and it must pass as undated. It is in black letter, and was printed, very inaccurately, from the edition of 1602, which it follows page for page. It is impossible to say whether it is earlier or later than the quarto of 1617, but is here treated as earlier, since that assumption has the double convenience of placing it next to its source and of keeping the four black-letter editions together. In what follows, therefore, this undated edition is called the fourth, and that of 1617 the fifth. The unique copy of this fourth edition (the peculiar interest of which will be explained later) was formerly in the Heber collection and later at Rowfant, and has recently been acquired by the University of Chicago Libraries. There are thus no less than five editions of this moral play : it will be observed that of these the first, second, and fifth agree page for page, and so do the third and fourth : it is also curious to note that while the first, third, and fourth survive, so far as is known, in a single copy each, there are at least four extant of the second and possibly twice that number of the fifth.

Evidence of the popularity of the piece may also be seen in the fact that five passages, one of some length, were quoted from it by Robert Allot in his anthology, *England's Parnassus*, 1600. Four are given over the name of Robert Greene, one over that of Doctor Lodge, but it is doubtful whether any weight can be attached to these ascriptions. The readings show that the quotations were taken from the edition of 1598, but there are a few peculiar variants, which will be found recorded in the list of readings below. The quotations are as follows.

Iustice. p. 155.
[= ll. 769–70]

Who paffeth iudgement for his priuate gaine,
He well may iudge he is adiudg'd to paine.
R. Greene.

Lechery. p. 164.
[= ll. 939–40]

Where whoredome raignes, there murder follows faft,
As falling leaues before the winters blaft.
R. Greene.

Pollicie. p. 240.
[= ll. 1812–3]

The head that deemes to ouertop the skie,
Shall perifh in his humane pollicie.
R. Greene.

Prayer. p. 242.
[= l. 2127]

Heauens are propitious vnto fearfull prayers.
R. Greene.

Of Tempests.
pp. 361–2.
[= ll. 1385–
1407]

- - - An hoaft of blacke and fable clouds
Gan to ecclipfe *Lucinaes* filuer face,
And with a hurling noyfe from forth the South,
A guft of winde did raife the billowes vp,

vii

Then fcantled we our failes with fpeedy hands,
And tooke our drablers from our bonners ftraine,
And feuered our bonnets from our courfes :
Our top failes vp we truffe, our fprite failes in,
But vainely ftriue they that refift the heauens,
For loe the waues incenfe then more and more,
Mounting with hideous rorings from the depth ;
Our Barke is battered by encountring ftormes,
And welnie fteemd by breaking of the clouds :
The fteeres-man pale, and carefull holds the helme,
Wherein the truft of life and fafety lay,
Till all at once, a mortall tale to tell,
Our failes were fplit by *Bifas* bitter blaft ;
Our middle broke, and we bereft of hope ;
There might you fee with pale and ghaftly lookes,
The dead in thought, and dolefull Marchant lifts
Their eyes and hands vnto their Country Gods,
The goods we caft in bowels of the Sea,
A facrifice to fwage proud *Neptunes* ire.

D. Lodge.

The present play is mentioned under the title of ' the lookingglasse' in Henslowe's Diary, as an old piece performed by Strange's men at the Rose on four occasions from 8 March to 7 June 1592. The receipts recorded varied from 7s. to 55s., and the play would thus seem to have exhausted its popularity on the stage before ever it came to be printed. The date of composition is uncertain, but it was most likely either 1588 or c. 1590. The Clown is called Adam, a name which also occurs in *James IV*, possibly as that of the actor who took the part of Oberon, and suggests that the original performer may have been John Adams, who was with the Queen's men in 1588. A Jonah comedy performed by English players at Nördlingen in 1605 may have had some connexion with the present piece. Some attempt has been made to distinguish the contributions of the two authors named on the title-page, but the result has not been very convincing.

LIST OF IRREGULAR, DOUBTFUL, AND VARIANT READINGS.

The editions of 1598, 1602, [n.d.], and 1617 are here referred to by the numerals 2, 3, 4, 5 respectively. (It should be borne in mind that 4 is Collins's Q 5, and 5 his Q 4.) While the succession of the editions, as already explained, is sufficiently clear, there are naturally many anomalous agreements due to chance coincidence of variation. The most striking is that in 1611, where *balme* was misprinted *blame* in 2, whence it was copied as *blame* in 5, while it was corrected to *balme* in 3, only to be again misprinted *blame* in 4. This instance also illustrates a general tendency: 3 containing quite a number of intelligent corrections, while 4 manifests excessive carelessness. None of the later editions, however, are of the least authority, and except in cases where the original text is corrupt, their readings possess no interest whatever. There would, indeed, have been no excuse for recording them here, had it not been for the fact that the elaborate apparatus included in Churton Collins's edition proved on examination to be completely misleading. No independent collation has been made for the present reprint (since no object would be served by multiplying instances of corruption in the later editions) but every variant recorded by Collins (together with a few from other sources) has been checked in each of the four later quartos. The absence from the ensuing list of any printed variant cited by Collins, means that that variant is imaginary. (His explicit assertions that in 157 the Bodleian and British Museum copies of 2 differ, and that in 175 the reading ‘ Cruch ’ is due to a ‘ *MS. correction in Q* 1 ’, are entirely without foundation.) Thus, although the list of variants here printed is certainly incomplete (4 in particular containing a number of unrecorded errors) it is hoped that so far as it goes it is accurate. Where several editions are cited as agreeing in a particular reading, the spelling given is, of course, that of the first cited, and may or may not be that of the others. Readings of the original edition (1594) certainly or probably incorrect are marked with an asterisk (*): an obelus (†) distinguishes readings or conjectures of modern editors and critics which are definitely to be rejected. Dyce is the only modern editor whose work on the text possesses any value as a whole, and only his second (revised) edition has been here taken into account. Except as regards spellings (which he modernized) and stage-directions (which he often recast) Dyce's readings (when not cited) may be assumed to derive from the original when this is unstarred, and when it is starred from a correction in a later quarto.

In the case of obvious literal errors and the like in the original, as a rule only the earliest quarto to make the correction is cited, followed by the sign +. If such an error persisted through all the quartos the correction has been given in parentheses, preceded by *read*; it being considered superfluous to cite modern editions. Otherwise the name of the first editor or critic to make or suggest an emendation is in each case given. Dyce's first text appeared in his edition of Greene's plays in 1831, his second in his joint edition of the plays of Greene and Peele in 1861. The text in the Hunterian Club edition of Lodge, 1878–82, vol. iv, is a mere unannotated reprint of the second quarto (1598). Grosart's text is in his complete edition of Greene, 1881–3, vol. xiv; Collins's in the first volume of his edition of Greene's plays, 1905. The facsimile issued by J. S. Farmer in 1914 was made from the edition of 1598, although it bears the date 1594 on the title. W. S. Walker's emendations will be found in his *Critical Examination of the Text of Shakespeare*, edited by W. N. Lettsom, 1860; K. Deighton's in his *Old Dramatists: Conjectural Emendations* (first series), 1896; and J. Le Gay Brereton's in his *Elizabethan Drama: Notes and Studies*, 1909 (in a review of Churton Collins's edition, reprinted from the *Beiblatt* to *Anglia* of 2 Feb. 1907). It may be mentioned, in conclusion, that the name *Rasni* is misprinted *Rasin* only (but consistently) in the outer forme of sheet A of the first edition. The possessive form, however, appears as *Rasnes* throughout the first edition, and was only corrected to *Rasnies* very sporadically in the later quartos. *Licas* or *Lycas* occurs consistently for *Licus* in all early editions. It should be added that in the black letter of the original two ligatures occur that have not been preserved in the present reprint: namely *oo* and *ée*, which have been replaced by separate and unaccented letters.

1 Enters] Enter *3, 4, Dyce*
   *Raſin] Raſni *2+*
   *Cicilia] Cilicia *5 (cf. 797)*
7 ꝑou] *omit. 4*
   anꝺ] are, *Dyce*
8, 11 *Raſins] Raſnies *2+*
   11 ercellence] ercellency *2–5*
   16 hundꝛeth] hundred *5, Dyce*
   17 *poꝛtople (*read* poꝛtaple)
   22 *poꝛalels (*read* paꝛalels)
   23 *to] *omit. 3, 4*
   26 Cades (*i.e.* Kadesh *or* Kedesh—*Vulgate*, Gen. xx. 1, Joshua xii. 22)
   27 Benhadab] Benhadad *4, Dyce* (*but unrevised Vulgate*, 3 Kings xv. 18, Benadab)

28 *brought, (*roman*)] bꝛougḥt, 2+
31 *Cicilia.] *Cilicia.* 5
35 Hiacynth] *Hyacinth* 5 : hyacinth *Dyce*
36 Nunpareile (*i.e.* nonpareil)
40 Mars] Mavors *Dyce* (*cf.* 506)
42 ḥaugḥtie] haught *Dyce*
44 Curteler (*i.e.* curtal-axe, cutlas)
46 tḥe] *omit.* 4
48 *wealth. (*roman*)] wealtḥ. 2+
49 peace] *omit.* 2-5
51 *Dania] Diana 3, 4 : Danäe *Dyce*
52] That Venus wait [*i.e.* waited] on with a golden shower *Walker*
       conj. (ii. 60)
53 ſtolne] ſtolen 2 : ſtole 4 : ſtollen 5
       *Raſnes] Raſnies 3, 4
54 tide (*i.e.* tied)
57 *Aluia] *Aluida* 5
58 bring] bringing 3-5, *Dyce*
60 Ioue] Ione 4
62 ſtroyes] strows *Dyce* (but perhaps = raze, level, the primary sense)
67 muſtering] blustering *Dyce conj.*
68 pines] Princes 4
       Libanon] *Lebanon* 5, Dyce
69 Iury] Iewry 3, 4, *Dyce*
70 Cades] Cade 3, 4 (*cf.* 26)
71 kinde] king 4
79 louely] lonely 4
85, 88 *Raſnes (*read* Raſnies)
89 *deeds ?] deeds, 2+
90 tḥou] tḥougḥ 2, 5
90-1] Wḥy ſḥould not fꝛom our royall ſoueraigntie ? *add.* 4
94 *Raſnes (*read* Raſnies)
98 by] my 3, 4, †*Dyce*
100 *darling,] darling 3, 4
101, 102 *Raſin] Raſni 2+
102 eitḥer] richer *Dyce conj.* : higher *Daniel conj.* (*apud Collins*) (*but
       the order is perhaps possible*)
104 weddings] wedding *Dyce*
106 Albia (*for* Albion)
111 *Raſins] Raſnies 2+
112 on] to 2-5

115 ſiſter] thy sister *Dyce conj.*
119 lowes (*i.e.* allows)] loues *2, 3, 5,* †*Dyce :* loue *4*
120 *Raſin] Raſni *2+*
123 ſiſters] ſiſter *4*
126 *Raſin] Raſni *2+*
    *within Radon] with him, Radagon *Dyce*
127 Sophiſtri] Sophiſtrie *4, 5*
129 *Radagon the] giue Radagon, thy *2 :* giue Radagon thy *3–5,*
    †*Dyce*
130 *thee] thou *Dyce :* the *Brereton conj.*
134 *quandam (*read* quondam)
137 *Remelias (*read* Remelia)
138 thy] my *2, 5 :* the *4*
139 Tis] This' (*i.e.* This is) *Dyce conj.*
    *Aluia (*read* Aluida)
140 *faire] a faire: *2, 5 :* faire: *3, 4 :* fair.—*Dyce*
    thaſt] thou haſt *2–5*
153 Whatſoeuer] Whate'er *Dyce*
157 Smith.] *omit. Dyce (warning for 192)*
    *Deneſum] Divisum *Dyce*
    *teneo] teno *4*
159 ſet] let *3, 4,* †*Dyce*
164 *Carnell] Calue *3, 4 : Carmell 5,* Dyce
175 Cruch] Church *2–5*
179 *through (*so* Dyce) thoghts *4*
181 the] *omit. 3, 4*
192 Enters] Enter *3–5,* Dyce
197 M.] Maiſter *3 :* Maſter *4 :* master *Dyce*
203 pettie] *omit. 3, 4*
213 youth, he was faith] youth he was faith, *2–5 :* youth he was,
    faith, *Dyce*
    *foure] †forty *Dyce* (*read* foure ſcore)
220 that] thou haſt *5*
222 oppropious] opprobrious *5,* Dyce
223 *D] Smith. D *3, 4 (within the line)*
226 a] of a *2–5*
229 Cuts,] colts, *4 : omit. 5*
230 thee] *omit. 4*
    ſhalt n⟨ot⟩ (*or* n⟨er⟩)] thou ſhalt *2, 3 :* thou ſhalt not *4, 5,* Dyce
232 *1. Clowne. (*read* Clowne.)
233 *A] Smith. A *3, 4*

239 *⟨That⟩ (see 2)] Smith. That 3, 4
243 *⟨Marrie⟩ (see 2)] Smith. Marrie 3, 4
247 spuing] spiuing 4 : Spauing 5 : spavin Dyce
     splent] Splene 4
     ring-bone] King bone 4
248 fashion (i.e. farcin, farcy)
253 *flouings] flouens 2–5
255 woe] wooe 3, woo 4, 5
258 *⟨No⟩w (see 2)] Smith. Now 3, 4
263 *⟨Th⟩e (see 2)] Smith. The 3, 4
     a (first)] omit. 3, 4
266 here] heue 4 : heare 5
267 is] it is 3, 4
272 *for] for a 2–5
273 (new paragraph anomalous)
277 *Why] Smith. Why 3, 4
281 *Lead] Clowne. Lead 3, 4
282 out] our 4
287 infant] Infants 5
290 Enters] Enter 3, 4, Dyce
292 these] those 2, 5, †Dyce
302 friends] men 4
306 *hast] so Dyce (read hast not)
309 sir] omit. 4
317 hand set (space doubtful)] hand set 2+
319 it] that 5
     deuise] deuice 2–4
330 thy] omit. 4
333 I] A 4
337 Strikes 4] It strikes 4. 3 : It strikes foure 4
341 counterpaine (i.e. counterpart)
354 goodly] pretie 2–5, †Dyce
     soape (i.e. sop)] sope 3–5 : †sup Dyce
409 gaine] gaines 4
410 pleasures is] pleasure is 4 : pleasures are Dyce
412 the] omit. 4
414 vtterly] vtterly is 4
427 Queenes] Queene 2–5, †Dyce
     handmaids] †handmaid Dyce
     *Rasnes] Rasnies 3, 4
430 *(line in roman)] (line in black letter) 3+

xiii

432 *Remilias (*read* Remilia)
433 Richt] Rich *2–5*
    excellence?] excellencie? *2 :* excellencie, *3, 4 :* excellence ; *5 :* excellence, *Dyce*
434 *shine.] shine? *2–4, Dyce :* shine : *5*
438 *eyne] eye *2–5*
439 *Anrera] Aurera *2 :* Aurora *3+*
441 *plac'st] placest *2 :* plac'd *3, Dyce :* placd *or* pla'd *4 :* plaste *5*
444 fro] from *2–5, Dyce :* 'fore *Dyce conj.*
447 richest] riches *2, 5*
450 paintings] painting *2–5*
452 lookes] dayes *5*
457 it trick and] and tricke it *5*
467 *Rasnes] Rasnies *3, 4*
477 I] he *2–5*
485 Aluida] I aluida *4*
486 *Th'assirian (*read* th'Assirian)
490 *il.] ill. *3–5 :* it. *Dyce*
491 How] Now *4*
496 tract] trac'd *3, 4*
    tender] *omit. 2–5*
503 straight] stright *2, 5*
506 *knancks] eunuchs *Dyce*
509 the place] her place *3, 4*
512 is] is the *4*
513 peny siluer (*space doubtful*)] pennie siluer *2+*
517 your] our *2, 5*
520 I . . . pomp.] on further pomp I will bethink me. *Dyce conj.*
    further] furth,a *2 :* such a *3–5*
522 their] her *3, 4*
526 *man] men *5*
534 and] or *2, 3, 5*
536 exalations] exalitations *2, 5 :* exaltations *4*
540 Inkindled] In kindling *2, 5 :* Enkindling *3, 4*
541 *Angurer] *Augurer 5*
548 wooe] wed *3, 4*
549 *Necternall (*read* Nocternall)
551 Remilia] Remilia is *3, 4*
553 vvith Thunder, blacke.] blacke with thunder. *3, 4, Dyce*
556 blent] bent *2–5*
557 of] from *5*

559 fetch herbes] herbes 4
568 Uiceroyes] Uiceroy 2, 3, 5
583 *Rasnes] rasnies 4 : *Rasnies* 5
587 *thrust] *thrusts* 5
      *Exeant] *Exeunt* 2+
592 wantons flie,] wanton flie, 2–5 (*read* wantons, flie) (*cf.* 765)
593 *seales] *so Dyce* : stales *C. E. Doble conj.* (*apud Collins*)
598 Prophets, we] (*couplet corrupt, Dyce*) Prophet's woe *J. C. Smith*
      conj. (*apud Collins*) : prophet, he *Collins conj.* : Prophet's ire
      Brereton conj.
599 After] And after *Collins conj.*
      exspect] expects *Collins conj.*
600 *Gentlemau] Gntleman 2 : Gentleman 3+
611 mease (*i.e.* mess)
626 goods] (*i.e.* god's)
630 her] he 2 : the 5, †*Dyce*
632 Knaue] and Knaue 2–5, *Dyce*
638 word] words 4
649 *aknee] a knee 2+
656 would] should 4
658 and] or *Dyce*
668 the other] an other 4
672 yet] *omit.* 5
      you] *omit.* 3, 4
682 wrong] wrongs 4
689 saies] sayeth 5
698 *keepe] kept 5, *Dyce* : keeps *Brereton conj.*
699 *trisle] trisle 2+
711 were] are 4
720 for] to 4
727 chawing] chewing 2–5, *Dyce*
730 *M. maister] M maister 4 : Maister 5, *Dyce*
739 thy] the 4
741 shuld] should 4, 5
750 (*Dyce adds an exit here, but the space implies no break*)
765 *Iudges flie, (*read* Iudges, flie) (*cf.* 592)
769 *passerh] passeth 2+
776 loue] loues 2–5, *Dyce*
782 daggar] dagger 2–5
784 *thee] thee. 2+
786 thou] to 2–5

xvi

935 myrre] muſke *4*
939 murther] murder *4, EP, Dyce*
940 winter] winters *EP*
942 regard] reward *2-5*
948 ſee] ſet *2-5*
      at] on *4*
953 teſtifie] to testify *Dyce*
954 mine] my *4*
957 thine] thy *4*
962 *inthroan'd] inthroan'd, *2-5* : enthron'd: *Dyce*
967 woe] woes *3, 4*
969, 970 contem'd] contemn'd *2-5*
975 Amithais] amithias *4* : Amittai's *Dyce* (Jonah i. 1; *but see*
      Bishops' Bible, 4 Kings xiv. 25)
981 *thſe] theſe *2+*
986 *Ionas] Ionas. *2+*
987 intending] attending *3, 4*
991 do] to *2, 5*
994 *ſinne] sins *Dyce*
1004 *fall] fall *2+* (fall *5*)
      *is, (*read* is.)
1005 flee] flie *3, 4, †Dyce*
1006, 1008 Tharſus (*i.e.* Tarshish : *Vulgate and Bishops' Bible,* Jonah i. 3,
      Tharsis *; perhaps confused with* Tarsus, Acts xi. 25)
1010 one] on *2-5*
1014 our] your *4*
1017 M.] Maiſter, *3, 4* : *Master,* Dyce
1018 *yonr (n *probably turned* u)] your *2+*
1022 *Orious (*read* Orions)
1024 Arcturus] Acturus *4*
1026 booke-men] booke-man *5*
1028 ſtir (*i.e.* steer)] steer *Dyce*
1032 none] not, *4*
1034 I] Ile *3-5*
1036 *flight,] flight. *3*
1046 thy] thine *2-5, †Dyce*
      I] Ile *3, 4*
1048 *To one] *so* Dyce : Go on *J. C. Smith conj. (apud Collins)*: To
      wone *Brereton conj.*
      faile] failes *3, 4, †Dyce (assuming lacuna)*
1053 or] of *4*

xvii   c

1055   foule] fold *2–5*
1067   𝔱𝔥𝔦𝔰] 𝔱𝔥𝔢 *4*
1070   *Alcon] Alcon. *2+*
1081   *𝔰𝔴𝔢𝔢𝔱𝔢] 𝔰𝔴𝔢𝔢𝔱 *2+*
1084   𝔣𝔬𝔬𝔩𝔦𝔰𝔥 𝔍 𝔱𝔬] 𝔣𝔬𝔬𝔩𝔦𝔰𝔥𝔩𝔶 𝔍 𝔡𝔬 *2, 3, 5* : 𝔣𝔬𝔬𝔩𝔦𝔰𝔥 𝔍 𝔡𝔬 *4*
1087   *𝔳𝔰.] 𝔳𝔰, *3, 4*
1090   *𝔗𝔥𝔬] 𝔗𝔥𝔢 *2+*
1091   𝔦𝔫𝔫𝔬𝔠𝔢𝔫𝔱𝔰] *omit.* *4*
1092   Solus (*cf.* 1131, 1138)] attended *Dyce*
1101   𝔠𝔬𝔪𝔢] 𝔠𝔬𝔪𝔢𝔰 *3, 4, Dyce*
1103   𝔭𝔯𝔢𝔰𝔢𝔫𝔱𝔩𝔶] *omit.* *3, 4*
1107   𝔥𝔞𝔱𝔥] *omit.* *4*
1110   𝔞𝔩𝔩] *omit.* *4*
1114   𝔦𝔫] 𝔱𝔬 *2–5*
1131   𝔶𝔬𝔲] 𝔶𝔢 𝔶𝔬𝔲 *2* : ye *5*
1136   𝔞𝔫𝔡] but *5, Dyce*
1138   Titius] *Tirius* *5* : 'Tityus' *Dyce*
1149   𝔥𝔞𝔲𝔫𝔱] 𝔡𝔞𝔲𝔫𝔱 *4*
1154   𝔰𝔥𝔬𝔲𝔩𝔡] 𝔰𝔥𝔞𝔩𝔩 *5*
1160   *𝔱𝔬, (*read* 𝔱𝔬.)
1164   𝔣𝔦𝔯𝔰𝔱] *omit.* *2–5*
1188   *𝔗𝔥𝔶] 𝔚𝔥𝔶 *2+*
1192   *Raſnes] raſnies *4* (*read* Raſnies)
1202   𝔙𝔦𝔩𝔩𝔞𝔦𝔫𝔢𝔰] 𝔙𝔦𝔩𝔩𝔞𝔦𝔫𝔢 *2, 5*
1204   𝔰𝔱𝔞𝔩𝔢𝔰] ſtalles *5*
1206   *𝔖𝔬] so *Dyce* : Too *J. C. Smith conj.* (*apud Collins*)
1207   *Raſnes . . . Raſnes (*read* Raſnies . . . Raſnies)
1216   𝔱𝔬𝔲𝔤𝔥𝔱] 𝔱𝔞𝔲𝔤𝔥𝔱 *3, 4*
1222   *Exet] *Exit* *2–5* (for *Exeunt*)
1226   𝔣𝔬𝔯] 𝔬𝔣 *2–5*
1232   *Exet] *Exi.* *2* : Exit *3+*
1235   𝔱𝔬𝔯𝔱𝔲𝔬𝔲𝔰] torturous *5*
1242   𝔣𝔩𝔞𝔪𝔢𝔰] 𝔣𝔩𝔞𝔪𝔟𝔢𝔰 *3, 4*
1244   *Th'aſſirian (*read* 𝔱𝔥'Aſſirian)
       Satrapos] Satropos *3* : Sairopos *4* (*for* Satrapes, satrap)
1249   *𝔪𝔦𝔯𝔞𝔠𝔲𝔩𝔬𝔲𝔰, (*read* 𝔪𝔦𝔯𝔞𝔠𝔲𝔩𝔬𝔲𝔰.)
1252   𝔟𝔢𝔩𝔬𝔴 (*possibly* 𝔟𝔢𝔩𝔬𝔴,)] 𝔟𝔢𝔩𝔬𝔴 *2, 4, 5* : 𝔟𝔢𝔩𝔬𝔴, *3*
1253   *Vulueus] Vulcans *4*
1257   *𝔮𝔲𝔦𝔱𝔢, (*read* 𝔮𝔲𝔦𝔱𝔢.)
1258   *Radagon.] Radagon, *3, 4*
1263   𝔠𝔬𝔲𝔯𝔱𝔦𝔫𝔤] 𝔠𝔬𝔲𝔢𝔱𝔦𝔫𝔤 *4*

1402 rudder] middle *EP*
1404 merchants] marchants *2, 5* : Marchant *EP*
 *lifts,] lifts *3, EP* : lift *Dyce*
1405 Countries] Country *EP*
1415 *come] came *3, 4*
1418 question] questions *3, 4*
1438 *perfume] fume *Dyce*
1439 gassampine] Cassampine *3, 4 (for* gossampine, cotton cloth)
1441 most] *omit. 3, 4*
1444 the] your *2–5*
1445 And] †Are *J. C. Smith conj. (apud Collins)*
 Exeunt a sacrifice.] a *Sacrifice.* | *Exeunt.* 5 : *Exeunt. A sacrifice.*
 Dyce (? read *Exeunt* to a sacrifice.)
1453 *paine.] paine, *4*
1463 hands . . . reares] hands . . . rear *Dyce*
1471 humble] †simple *Grosart*
 stresse (*i.e.* straining)] †stretch *Dyce conj., Grosart*
 *chappes,] so *Dyce, Grosart* : chappes *Collins*
1480 hadst] haft *5*
1483 my] thy *2–4*
1490 The] An *3, 4*
1494 Depart Angell.] The Angel departs. *3, 4, Dyce*
1495 *Priest] prest *5*
1499 *towns] towres *5*
1500 thy] the *2–5*
 pride of] of proud *3, 4*
1503 commands] commaund *3, 4*
1504 *Exet.] *Exit.* 2+*
1510 her] and her *3, 4, Dyce*
1515 Thou] Tho *2, 5*
1516 Enter] *Enters 5*
1517 Cilicia,] Cilicias *2–5*
1523 *Rasnes (*read* Rasnies)
1528 *thee faire,] thee faire *2–5 (read* thee, faire)
1530 *me:] me? *3, 4* : me. *Dyce*
1535 *iest,] iest. *3, 4*
1536 rest] iest *3, 4*
1537 *Song.]* The Song. *3, 4* : *Sings Dyce*
1544 *Fairer] Fairest *Walker conj.* (i. 59) : (? read Fair art)
 I (*i.e.* ay)] I *Dyce*
1546 *plant] so *Dyce* : pant *Grosart*

1557   **foꝛ my**] for his *Dyce*
1560   Embrace] She imbraceth *3, 4*
1561   Cinthias] Cithias *2–5*
       Pheere (*roman*)] **Spheere** *3, 4* (*read* **Pheere**)
1564   Embrace] She embraceth *3, 4*
1566   Kiſſe.] She kiſſeth him. *3, 4*
1568   **wakeſt** (*for* wakedst)] wak'dst *Dyce*
1570   Kiſſe him.] She kiſſeth him againe. *3, 4*
1571   **you**] ye *Dyce* (*for rime*)
1572   **falc'd**] fale'd *4*
1576   Faints. Point] She faints, and points *3, 4 : Faints. Points 5*
1578   *****What**] Raſni. **What** *3, 4*
1579   **Whereon** (*possibly* **Where on**)] **Whereon** *2+*
1580   **motoꝛs**] **metoꝛs** *3, 4 :* meteors *5*
       my] the *5*
       *****woꝛld,**] **woꝛld.** *3+*
1581   *****axier** (*for* axis *Dyce:* or for ax-tre *NED*)
1583   *****the woꝛld**] my world *Dyce*
1585   as] *omit. 4*
1587   **thee?** (original **thee:**)
1588   Embrace] She embraceth *3, 4*
1589   **may**] *omit. 3, 4*
1593–5 †*assign to Alvida, W. N. Lettsom conj.* (*apud Walker,* i. 59)
1594   *****futes** Spenori] suits his pennons *J. Mitford conj.* (*apud Dyce*) :
       sumd his pennons *W. N. Lettsom conj.* (*apud Walker,* i. 59) (*but
       pennon for* pinion *is a blunder originating with Milton*)
1596   *****Galbocia**] Galatea *Dyce*
1599   *****creſt:**] **creſt,** *4*
1600   *****Onoris** (*read* Orions)
1610   **blend** (*i.e.* disturb, break, *cf.* 556, 961)
1611   **thy balme**] **thy blame** *2, 4, 5 :* my balm *Dyce*
1612   **while**] **when** *4*
1614   *****Morane**] Morn *Dyce*
1616   *****Catnies**] Catnies, *2–5 :* Caitiffs *Dyce* (*read* **Catiues**)
1617   Prieſt] Prieſts *3, 4, Dyce* (*cf.* 1620)
       vvith the miters (*? read* vvith the Sages, miters—*cf.* 1619, 1621,
       1640–1)
1619   *****Th'aſſirian** (*read* **th'**Aſſirian)
1622   **addittes** (*i.e.* adyta, inner shrines)
1623   *****warre.**] **warre** : *3 :* warre, *5*
1624   *****ghoſt**] ghoſts *5*

1625   this] the 4
1626   statutes (*for* statues)] statues 4, 5, *Dyce*
      are throwne (*? read* are all throwne—*unless* throwne *is dissyllabic*)
1631   *tempteth] *so Dyce* (*but?*)
1632   doores] walles 2-4: wals 5
1633   binde me] blinde the 4
1636   threatneth] threatning with 3, 4 : threatens *Dyce*
1642   *retrograde, (*roman*)] retrograde 3+
1644   *radiatrous (*read* radiations)
1645   kindled (*? read* enkindled—*unless* Spheare *is dissyllabic*)
1659   warnings profit] warning profits 4
1661   one] on 2-5
1677   pound] pounds 4
1695   Spritus fantus] Spiritus fantus 3, 4
1698   Nominus patrus (*sic*)
1705   muft thou] thou muft 5
1715   a thruft] athirst *Dyce* (*but* athruft *is a possible form*)
1716   fpirits] a fpirit 4
1722   *you,] you. 5
1723   hath] he hath 4
1724   fpritus fantus] fpiritus fantus 4
      nominus patrus (*sic*)
1733   dare] dares 5
1739   it] that (y^t) *Dyce conj.*
1745   (*entrance needed*)
1759   a] *omit.* 3, 4
1760   let vs] lets 5
1761 c.w. *Diuell. (*repeated from recto*)] Vfurer. 2+
1764   a] and a *Dyce*
1766   M.] Maifter 3 : Mafter 4, *Dyce*
1780   Repent (*read* Ionas. Repent)
1781   horror and of torment] iudgement 2, 3, 5 : iudgements 4
1784   *bane. (*read* bane,)
1785   *hell. (*read* hell,)
1786   *rewarded. (*read* rewarded,)
1796-1800, 1803 *Exet.] Exit. 2+
1802   *punifh] punifheth 4 : doth punifh *Dyce*
1804   with] and 4
1815   *youth. (*read* youth,)
1817   powle (*i.e.* poll, plunder)
      the pride] *omit.* 4

(1817) *-weale ?] -weale. *3* : -weale, *4*
1818   laborinth] Labyrinth *5, Dyce*
1819   *life. (*read* life,)
1821   *holie. (*read* holie,)
1822   ſhall] ſhould *2–5*
        they] it *4*
1823   *neare,] near : *Dyce*
1827   𝔢𝔦𝔢𝔰] eye *Dyce*
1837   𝔱𝔥𝔢ſ𝔢] 𝔱𝔥𝔢 *4*
1847   her] *omit. 2–5*
1851   *𝔅𝔬𝔯𝔞𝔠𝔥𝔦𝔬𝔲𝔰] 𝔅𝔬𝔯𝔞𝔠𝔥𝔦𝔫𝔰 *4* : borachios *Dyce*
1854   *𝔱𝔬] but to *Dyce*
1860   ſ𝔨𝔦𝔫𝔠𝔨 (*i.e.* fill, *properly* pour)] ſ𝔨𝔦𝔫𝔠𝔨𝔱 *2–4*
        𝔴𝔦𝔱𝔥] 𝔬𝔣 *2–5*
1861   𝔴𝔥𝔬𝔩𝔢] 𝔣𝔲𝔩𝔩 *2–5*
1867   𝔏.] 𝔏𝔬𝔯𝔡. *2, 3* : 𝔏𝔬𝔯𝔡, *4, 5* : lord, *Dyce*
1872   Aluida] heavenly Alvida *Dyce conj.*
1874   𝔥𝔢𝔞𝔲𝔢𝔫𝔩𝔶] *omit. Dyce conj.*
1877   *Raſnes] Raſnies *3–5*
1884   *𝔣𝔩𝔞𝔲𝔢] 𝔣𝔩𝔞𝔲𝔢 *2+*
1891   *𝔎𝔦𝔫𝔤. (*read* 𝔎𝔦𝔫𝔤 ?)
1897   *𝔩𝔞𝔫𝔡 ?] 𝔏𝔞𝔫𝔡, *3, 4*
1902   *Raſni,] Raſni. *2+*
        𝔴𝔥𝔞𝔱] *omit. 4*
1905   𝔍] Yea *5*
1915   𝔭𝔬𝔯𝔱 𝔯𝔶𝔲𝔞𝔩𝔢 (*i.e.* port rivel, *a landing-place, or ? a river port*)] 𝔭𝔬𝔯𝔱
        𝔯𝔶𝔲𝔞𝔩𝔱 *3, 4* : Port-Ryuale *5* : †port-royal *Dyce*
1920   *ſprytus ſantus* (sic)
1929   𝔣𝔬𝔯𝔴𝔞𝔯𝔡] goe forwards *5*
1933   𝔱𝔥𝔞𝔱] this *5*
1936   𝔴𝔞𝔫𝔱 𝔫𝔬] not vvant *5*
1938   𝔱𝔥𝔦𝔰] 𝔱𝔥𝔢 *4*
1940   𝔬𝔲𝔱 𝔬𝔣] 𝔣𝔯𝔬𝔪 *2–5*
1942   𝔴𝔞𝔰 𝔫𝔬] 𝔦𝔰 𝔫𝔬 *3, 4*
1948   *𝔣𝔞ſ𝔱𝔦𝔫] 𝔣𝔲ſ𝔱𝔦𝔫 *2, 3, 4* : fuſten *5* : fustian *Dyce*
1954   𝔄] 𝔍 *2–5*
        𝔥𝔞𝔯𝔡𝔦𝔢] 𝔥𝔞𝔯𝔱𝔦𝔢 *2–5, Dyce*
        *Ioue,] Ioue *2, 3*
1956   *𝔏𝔬𝔯𝔡] lords *Dyce*
1958   *𝔥𝔬𝔴] 𝔴𝔥𝔞𝔱 *2–5*
1963   *𝔴𝔥𝔞𝔱 𝔠𝔬𝔪𝔢] 𝔴𝔥𝔞𝔱 𝔠𝔬𝔪𝔢, *3–5* : What, come, *Dyce*

xxiii

1970   𝕽epent, repent,] Repent, *Dyce* (*cf.* 1780)

1971   ſpoken, and] ſpoken *4* : spoke, and *Dyce* (*cf.* 2003)

1976   *alarams] alarums *3–5*

1988   thy boundes,] the world. *4*

1990   *hoſte] hoſts *4*

1996   foe] foes *4*

2000   *Lamana.] Lamana, *Dyce* (*noting corruption*): †Gomorrah, *Grosart* : †El Adama, *Deighton* : Samaria, *J. C. Smith conj.* (*apud Collins*)

2001   thy] the *4*

2006   *Exet offered.] *Exit.* Offered. *2, 5* : Exit offered. *3, 4*

2009   *Exet.] *Exit.* *2+*

2015   *Exet. His Sages.] *Exit.* His Sages. *2:* Exit his Sages. *3, 4: Exit Sages. 5*

2019   *omit. 4*

2026   *Exet. A man.] *Exit.* A man. *2:* Exit a man. *3, 4: Exit. 5*

2027   ſhame] ſorrow *3, 4*

2041–2   (*but cf.* 2064–5)

2041   *ſolus*] alone *3, 4*

2046   *noughts] *so Dyce:* noughte *4*

2048   *me.] me, *3+*

2052   *Jle] all *Dyce*

2058   *Atna] etna *4: Ætna 5*

2068   Then (*possibly* Theu)] Theu *2:* Then *3+*

2069   *Mee-things] Mee-thinke, *2:* Mee-thinkes *3+*

2078   ſack-cloathes] sackcloth *Dyce*

2080   diſpiearſed] diſpierſed *2:* diſpearſed *3, 4: diſperſed 5*
      *lookes] locks *Dyce*

2081   brodred] broydred *3, 4*

2082   diſpiearſed] diſpierſed *2:* diſpearſed *3, 4:* diſperſed *5*

2084   ſackcloaths] sackcloth *Dyce*

2089   *fal,e (*read* falſe)] fall, *2, 5:* fall *3, 4:* false *Dyce :* †frail *Brereton conj.*

2095   fall] fals *5*

2097   *thinkes] think *Dyce*

2101   *Lord.] Lords. *3, 4: omit. Dyce* (*there is no Lord on*)

2104   *Kings] *King* Grosart

2106   ſo] *omit. 3, 4*

2111   *ſubiect] subject's *Dyce*

2113   laborinth] Labyrinth *5, Dyce*

2120   the … the] thy … thy *2–5*

2122   ſtreame] flow *Dyce conj.*

2127 *p?epitious] p?opitious 3+ (EP)
    faithful] fearfull EP
2136 *tent] teat 3, 4
2140 ⦱ pitie] pittie 4
2143 *fo?ie fo?ie] fo?ie 2–5: †sorry Dyce: †sore sorie Deighton and
       C. E. Doble (apud Collins) (read is fo?ie—fo?ie being a mar-
       ginal correction for fo?ie which has replaced the wrong word)
2147 p?aiers] p?aier 4
    require] requires 3, 4
    truce? (query doubtful)] truce? 2+
2149 temples] temple Dyce conj.
2151 Enters] Enter 3, 5
    folus] alone 3, 4
2156 watery] omit. 4
2158 Thefe] The 4, 5
2166 leaud] lewd 5, Dyce
2173 pleafant] fp?eading 4
2174 *heate,] heate. 3, 4
2175 omit. 4
2183 and of] and 2–5
2186 *noughts] nought 3, 4
2192 am] do 4
2195 plungde (i.e. overwhelmed, cf. 1113)
2197 *it?] it. 2, 5: it: 3, 4
2199 *Cariculer] canicular Dyce
2201 reft] rost (i.e. roast) Brereton conj.
2202 Ionas] omit. 5
2207 dide (i.e. died)
2209 wo?ld] Lo?d 2–5
2212 befide] befides 2–5
2218 *Exet] Exit 2+
2228 *life.] life 4 (read life,)
2232 fp?ight] fp?ing 4
2237 flop] fhop 2
2241 read-herings cob] red Herings cob 3–5: red-herring-cob Dyce
2244 fo] omit. 3, 4
2258 *Enters] Enter 3, 4
2261 as yet] omit. 4
2286 *necet] nocet 5
2297 in] in a 5
2305 fo] omit. 2, 5

2306 to you] *omit. 3, 4*

2310 am] am forry *5*

2311 𝕮𝖍𝖗𝖔𝖓𝖎𝖈𝖑𝖊𝖘.] 𝕮𝖍𝖗𝖔𝖓𝖎𝖈𝖑𝖊𝖘. *Exeunt. 3, 4,* Dyce

2312 *kings] king *3–5*
      *attended] attĕded. *2:* attended. *3, 5:* attending *4*

2314 𝖘𝖒𝖔𝖙𝖍𝖊𝖉] 𝖘𝖒𝖔𝖔𝖙𝖍𝖊𝖉 *2–5*

2316 *Imence] incense *Dyce*
      *𝕷𝖔𝖗𝖉 :] 𝕷𝖔𝖗𝖉, *3, 4*

2320 𝖋𝖔𝖗] 'fore *Dyce*

2321 *𝖍𝖆𝖚𝖊] 𝖍𝖆𝖙𝖍 *4, 5*

2328 *𝖍𝖔𝖘𝖙𝖊] hosts *Dyce*

2330 *𝖆𝖜𝖗𝖞,] 𝖆𝖜𝖗𝖞 *3, 4*

2336 𝖆] 𝖙𝖍𝖞 *2–5*

2340 𝖆𝖘] *omit. 4*

2341 c.w. 𝕿𝖍𝖊 (*to a lost line*)] 𝕴 𝖜𝖎𝖑𝖑 *2, 5 (3, 4 not end of page)*

2342] 𝕴 𝖜𝖎𝖑𝖑 𝖙𝖍𝖔𝖚 𝖕𝖗𝖆𝖈𝖙𝖎𝖘𝖊 𝖌𝖔𝖔𝖉𝖓𝖊𝖘𝖘𝖊, 𝖙 𝖛𝖊𝖗𝖙𝖚𝖔𝖚𝖘𝖓𝖊𝖘𝖘𝖊, *2–5*
      *𝖌𝖔𝖔𝖉𝖚𝖊𝖘𝖘𝖊, (𝖚 *perhaps turned* 𝖓—*read* 𝖌𝖔𝖔𝖉𝖓𝖊𝖘𝖘𝖊,)] †good is *Dyce*
      (*see 2341*)

2347 𝖙𝖔] *omit. 4*

2350 𝖎𝖓] *omit. 4*

2351 𝖆𝖘] 𝖔𝖓 *4*
      *Lepher] Sepher *Dyce conj.* (*see Vulgate and Bishops' Bible,* Num.
      xxxiii. 23–4; *but it was a mountain*)

2352 𝖔𝖋𝖘𝖕𝖗𝖎𝖓𝖌] 𝖔𝖋𝖘𝖕𝖗𝖎𝖓𝖌𝖘 *2–5*

2354 𝖜𝖎𝖙𝖙𝖎𝖓𝖌𝖑𝖞] 𝖜𝖎𝖑𝖑𝖎𝖓𝖌𝖑𝖞 *4*

2359 𝖍𝖆𝖚𝖊] 𝖍𝖆𝖙𝖍 *4*
      𝖉𝖊𝖙𝖆𝖎𝖓𝖉] 𝖗𝖊𝖙𝖆𝖎𝖓𝖉 *2–4:* retainde *5*

2363 𝖋𝖔𝖗𝖊] 𝖋𝖔𝖗𝖙𝖍 *2, 5*

2366 *𝖎𝖚 (𝖚 *perhaps turned* 𝖓)] in *2+*

2384 Actean (*i.e.* coastal, Attic)] Acteon *3–5*

2391 *𝖆𝖌𝖊.] 𝖆𝖌𝖊, *3–5*

2392 *𝖕𝖔𝖔𝖗𝖊 :] 𝖕𝖔𝖔𝖗𝖊 ; *4 (read* 𝖕𝖔𝖔𝖗𝖊,*)*

2396 *𝖓𝖊𝖎𝖌𝖍𝖇𝖔𝖗𝖘 𝖇𝖚𝖗𝖓𝖘] neighbour burnes *5:* neighbours burn *Dyce :*
      neighbor burns *Collins*

2399 𝖉𝖔] 𝖉𝖔𝖙𝖍 *3, 4*

2402 𝕼𝖚𝖊𝖊𝖓𝖊] King *5*

2406 𝖘𝖍𝖊] he *5*

2408 *𝖔𝖚𝖊𝖗𝖘𝖍𝖊𝖆𝖉] overshade *Dyce*
      𝖍𝖊𝖗] his *5*

LIST OF CHARACTERS

in order of their appearance.

RASNI, King of Nineveh, or of Assyria.
The King of CILICIA.
The King of CRETE.
The King of PAPHLAGONIA.
RADAGON, a courtier, son of Alcon.
REMILIA, sister to Rasni.
ALVIDA, wife of Paphlagonia.
an Angel.
OSEAS, the prophet, as Chorus.
a Smith.
ADAM, a clown, his man.
two Ruffians.
a Usurer.
THRASIBULUS, a young gentleman.
ALCON, a poor man.
Magi.

a Lawyer.
a Judge.
a Lord.
JONAS, the prophet.
a Master Mariner.
a Sailor.
a Merchant of Tharsus.
SAMIA, wife of Alcon.
CLESIPHON, their son.
the Smith's wife.
The Governor of JOPPA.
The Priest of the Sun.
a man disguised as a Devil.
an Evil Angel.
Ladies.
two Searchers.

Lords, Ladies, Ruffians, Sailors, Merchants.

The King of Cilicia is miscalled Cicilia on his first appearance (1, 31). Jonas is, of course, the Vulgate form of Jonah, which survived in the Bishops' Bible. Oseas is evidently the prophet Hosea, the form of the name being perhaps due to mistaken analogy with Jonas: he is Osee ('Ωσηέ) in the Vulgate. The form Oseas occurs, however, in the Apocrypha, 4 (2) Esdras, i. 39, Bishops' Version (also Geneva and A.V.). The Smith's man (see below) appears in sc. iii, but it is not till sc. x that he is called Adam in the text, and not till sc. xiv that the name appears in the directions. His 'mistresse' in sc. xiv (with the prefix 'Wife') is, of course, the Smith's wife. The Young Gentleman and the Poor Man appear in sc. iv and again in sc. vi, but first acquire their names Thrasibulus and Alcon in sc. ix. In sc. xx the former is simply Gentleman in the direction, though he retains his name as a speaker. The Magi, Soothsayers, and Sages are, no doubt, all the same : they are mute on their first appearance as Magi in sc. v, a Soothsayer speaks in sc. ix, and Sages have a speech in sc. xiii. In the latter scene it is not certain whether there is more than one Priest of the Sun present (see List of Readings) but only one speaks.

There is one contradiction for which the authors are evidently responsible, and which is probably a result of collaboration. After the dismissal of the King of Crete in sc. i (129–34), he reappears without explanation in sc. xvi (1871, 1873). Dyce duly observed the oversight : ' Did the author forget here that the King of Crete had been banished by Rasni ? ' To which Grosart : ' But Rasni recalled the sentence.' Which is untrue.

There is a far worse confusion, a confusion which it is impossible wholly to clear up, in sc. iii. To begin with, the original edition (followed by Q 2 and Q 5) omits the speaker's name in eight places (see List of Readings). In the first seven it should clearly be ' Smith ', in the last ' Clown '. These were duly supplied in Q 3 (and Q 4). Now the speakers in this scene are : Smith, Clown, Ruffian, and 2 [Ruffian?]. (' 1. Clowne ' is presumably the same as the Clown elsewhere, though it suggests some confusion between Clowns and Ruffians.) But the stage-direction only mentions ' the Clowne and his crew of Ruffians ' and the crew certainly does not include the Smith. Moreover, the name ' Smith ' was evidently added (as a warning) in the margin of the manuscript from which the first quarto was printed, for it got in erroneously as a speaker's name before line 157. But the Smith in this scene is evidently not the Smith of the later scenes but his man Adam, since he speaks (197) of having left his master at the forge, and this is borne out by what the real Smith says later (844–7). We have, therefore, in this scene a Smith (= Smith's man) and a Clown who is the leader of a crew of Ruffians. But elsewhere (scs. vii, x, xiv, xvi, xix) the Clown is the Smith's man Adam, and in sc. vii (844) the Smith explicitly claims the ' Clowne ' as his ' man ' when he comes out of the ale-house to which he resorted as ' Smith ' at the end of sc. iii. Moreover, it will be noticed that at line 223 the ' Smith ' (= Smith's man) addresses the Clown as Peter, whereas later on the Clown's name is, of course, Adam. It is evident, therefore, that the authors began the play with the idea of having two Clown-parts, and finding later on that they could not afford them were compelled to amalgamate the characters. The confusion evidently caused trouble on the stage, for in the manuscript corrections in Q 4 (see below) it has been cleared up by the simple method of substituting the prefix Clown for Smith, and distributing the Clown's speeches between 1 and 2 Ruffian. Dyce achieved the same end by substituting Adam for Smith in this scene and for Clown elsewhere, and retaining Clown in this scene only.

The unique copy of the fourth edition, now at Chicago, has certain peculiar features which merit description here. As already explained, it has lost the title-leaf, in place of

which an eighteenth-century hand has supplied a manu-
script title which runs as follows : ' A | Looking Glasse
for | London and England | Tr: Com: | Geo: – – By – –
Smyth | Thos Lodge & Robt Green | [1598]' (the date has
been subsequently crossed out). George Smith was a consider-
able dramatic collector, and this quarto was lot 1174 in his
sale, which began on 2 June 1797, and at which it was bought
by Heber for 4s. 9d. Its interest lies in the fact that some
time in the first half of the seventeenth century it was used
as a prompt book and contains not only certain corrections
and alterations in the text, but also a number of prompter's
directions and notes. It is not clear whether these are all in
one hand : several styles of writing appear, but it is difficult
to differentiate them with certainty. The light brown ink is
said not to differ much in colour. On the other hand, there
is little doubt that the more roughly written are in a hand
that appears, as one of several, making similar notes in some
of the plays in MS. Egerton 1994 at the British Museum,
notably in *Edmond Ironside* and *The Two Noble Ladies*. The
notes in the quarto, however, are on the whole more care-
ful and probably earlier. Only one actor's name appears,
namely 'mr Reason '. This was without doubt Gilbert
Reason, who was a member of Prince Charles's company
from 1610 to 1625, and appears to have led a section of
it in the provinces at least as early as 1613. He is shown
as playing the Priest of the Sun (line 1617), but as a leading
member no doubt filled some more important part as well.
It is natural to suppose that it was in the country rather
than in London that this old play was acted. Appended is
a list of all the manuscript markings, compiled from photographs and most obligingly verified and corrected from the
original by Professor C. R. Baskervill, who has himself
published a minute description of the quarto in *Modern
Philology* (1932, xxx. 29–51).

List of Manuscript Alterations and Additions in the Unique Copy of the Fourth Quarto

The signatures refer to the pages of the fourth edition, the line numbers to the present reprint of the first. The words *add r. (l.)* mean that the addition is written to right or left, either in the margin or in the space left by an incomplete line: *middle* that it is written in the middle in a space within the line or between lines: *foot* that it is written in the bottom margin below the line given. Again, *dele* means that the specified words of the text have been crossed out: *for* means that the first reading has been substituted for the second, usually by crossing out the one and writing the other in the margin. It should be borne in mind that the readings of the fourth quarto do not always agree with those of the first; also that the page division is usually different. Intended omissions are indicated in the original by a rule drawn down the left margin. Many of the additions have rules either below, above and below, or all round them.

A2 H.T. *add r.* $\frac{a}{g}$ *(this may be a later mark: it is repeated to the left of the lace ornament at the head of the page)*
    1 *add l. and above* fflorish.
A2ᵛ 47 *add r.* here.
    48 *add r.* Ent.
    49 *add l.* ×
       add r. Enter
    56 *add r.* +
A3 73 *add r.* —×pty *(uncertain)*
A3ᵛ 118 *add. l.* rada (Q 4 *prefix* ra.)
A4 136 *add r.* Exit.
    157 *add l.* fflorifh.
       add r. Clear
A4ᵛ 191 *add r.* clear
    194 *add l.* 1
    197 *[apparently left unaltered]*
    200 *add l.* 1 Ruf
    202 *add l.* clo
    205 1 Ruff *for* Clowne.
    206 *add l.* Clo

B1 221 1 Ruff *for* Clown.
    223 Clo *for* Smith. (Q 4 *within line: the alteration is both written over the original word and added in the left margin)*
    232 2 Ruff *for* I. Clowne.
    233 clo *for* Smith
    238 1 Ruf *for* Clowne.
    239 clo *for* Smith.
    242 2 Ruf *for* clowne.
    243 *add l.* clo
B1ᵛ 256 1 Ruff *for* Clowne.
    258 *add l.* Clo.
    262 2 Ruff *for* Clowne
    263 clo *for* Smith.
    276 2 Ruff *for* Clowne
    277 clo *for* Smith
    281 *add l.* 1 Ruff
       add r. Exeunt
       add foot Clear.
B2ᵛ 337 *add l.* ftrike.
B3 383 *add r.* —Exit
B3ᵛ 403 *add middle* clear.

(B3ᵛ) 424–5 *add l.* En (*with rule across the page above* S.D., *there being no space*)
B4ᵛ 504 *add foot* muſick.
C1 509 *add r.* muſick.
512–3 *add r.* Arbor riſes
514–28 *marked for omiſsion and crossed off*
518 *add r.* Lightning
519 *add l.* thunder.
522 *add r.* +
525–30 *add r.* Ent: Raſ: | Lords & magi | not paph:
530 *add l.* Thunder.
C1ᵛ 578 rad. *for* ra. (*prefix in* Q 4)
C2 584 rad. *for* ra. (*prefix in* Q 4)
586 *add r.* Clear.
587 *add l.* fflorifh :
C4 748 *add r.* —Ex.
763 *add r.* Clear
764 *add foot* Ofeas. (*warning*)
C4ᵛ 790 *add r.* Exit.
797 *add l.* fflorifh.
797–8 *dele* and of Pa-|phla-gonia
D1 829 Lord *for* alui.
835 Lord *for* alui.
add foot Verte Ent (*warning for* 840)
D1ᵛ 841 *add l.* Cilicia.
861–2 *add r.* ×
863 *add l.* Ent:
D2ᵛ 918 *add r.* Wyne.
937 (*for* 938) *add r.* cler.
938–9 *add l.* fflorifh.
D4 1050 *add r.* Clear
E1ᵛ 1151 *add l.* fflorifh.
magi. *for* Soothfayers
E2ᵛ 1229–30 *add r.* Lightning. & bolt

(E2ᵛ) 1231 *add l.* finke.
E3ᵛ 1270 *add r.* Clear
1271 *add l.* fflorifh.
E4 1309–10 *add l.* Ent:
1310 *add r.* Ent: Smith.
E4ᵛ 1358–9 *add middle* clear
F1ᵛ 1445 *add foot* Clear.
F2 1460 *add r.* whale
F2ᵛ 1487–8 *add r.* Ent: Angell
1503 *add r.* Clear
1510 *add l.* bowre.
F3 1538–9 *add r.* fong.
F3ᵛ 1574 *add l.* fflorifh. (*deleted*)
1596–7 *add l.* Ent: Rafn:| Creet : magi (*with a rule between the lines*)
1597 magi. *for* Lords.
F4 1615 *add r.* muficke (*deleted*)
1616 *add r.* thunder
1617 mʳ Reafon. *interlined with caret after* fun
F4ᵛ 1630 *add r.* here fword.
1634–5 *add r.* a burning fword.
1653 *add r.* cleare
1654 *add l.* fflorifh—
G2 1735 *add r.* Exeunt. clear
1741–2 *add r.* ×
1743–4 *add. r.* Ent: Alcon and | famia. Clefi:
1756 *add r.* Ent. Vfu: (*warning*)
1761 *add foot* Ent: Vfurer
G2ᵛ 1778–9 *add l.* Ent: to em
G3 1803 *add r.* Clear.
G3ᵛ 1845–6 *add r.* clear.
1846–7 *add l.* fflorifhe.
1847–9 *add l.* Cicilia. (*sic*) | Creete. | Attend:
G4 1881, 1884, 1888 *add l.* +
1891 *add l.* Cilicia.
H1 1953, 1955 *add r.* +d (*i.e. drinks*)

(H1) 1969 *add l.* Ent:
H2 2019 *in place of this line, omitted in* Q 4, *the following is written down the right margin :* that all the fubiectҽ [of my] to oʳ foveraigntie, (of my *being crossed out and* to oʳ *interlined with caret*)
    2024-5 *add r.* ☉
    2037-8 *add r.* ☉
    2039 *add r.* clear.
H3 2099-2103 *marked for omission*
    2101 *dele* lords.
    2105 *add l.* ☉
H3ᵛ 2128-35 *marked for omission*
    2140-2 (*to* 𝔥𝔢𝔞𝔲𝔢𝔫) *marked for omission*
    2150 *add foot* clear.
H4 2168 *add r.* Sunne
    2173 *add r.* Vine
    2178-9 *add r.* Serpent
    2128 *add foot* Serpent (*deleted*)
H4ᵛ 2189 *add r.* Serpent (*deleted*)
I1 2236 *add r.* —Exit / clear

I2 2311-2 *add l.* Ent:
    add r. clear.
I3 2376 *marked for omission*
    2388-90 *marked for omission. Down the right margin are written three lines apparently for substitution :* thou famous Citty London, cheif of all theis bleſt vnited nations do containe, more finne, in thee. then niniuy remaines.
    2391 *dele* 𝔠𝔬𝔫𝔱𝔢𝔪𝔭𝔱 𝔬𝔣 𝔊𝔬𝔡
    2395-8 *marked for omission*
    2399 *dele* 𝔣𝔬𝔯 𝔣𝔢𝔞𝔯𝔢 𝔱𝔥𝔢 𝔏𝔬𝔯𝔡 𝔡𝔬𝔱𝔥 𝔣𝔯𝔬𝔴𝔫𝔢, (*indistinct*)
    2401 frō thy fin *for* 𝔱𝔬 𝔱𝔥𝔢 𝔏𝔬𝔯𝔡,
    2402-3 *marked for omission*
    2406 𝔥𝔢 *for* 𝔱𝔥𝔢 (𝔱 *deleted*) build *for* 𝔟𝔦𝔡𝔢
    2408 𝔥𝔦𝔰 *for* 𝔥𝔢𝔯 (𝔢𝔯 *altered*)

In view of the fact that the two leaves B 2 and B 3 are defective in the only known copy of the first edition, reprints of the four corresponding pages in the second edition have been included at the end of the present text.

The first eight collotype plates that follow illustrate the quartos of 1594, 1598, 1602, and 1617. The last four are from the unique copy of the fourth edition (undated) and show some of the manuscript annotations.

The thanks of the Society are due to the authorities of the Huntington Library for permission to print the play from photographs of the unique original in their possession, to Mr. C. K. Edmonds for checking doubtful points in the same, and to Professor C. R. Baskervill for drawing the editor's attention to the copy of the fourth quarto at Chicago, and procuring a set of photographs for his use.

ERRATA

A few errors have crept into the reprint. There is in the original a curious convention, followed with almost perfect consistency, whereby in black letter a single hyphen (-) is used in compound words within the line, and a double hyphen (꞊) in words divided at the end of the line. Unfortunately this distinction escaped notice till after the first three sheets (A–C) had been printed off. The following corrections should therefore be made:

81	ſun-god	483	ſea-𝔑ymphs
112	hand-maides	520	𝔐eane-while,
212	mee-thinks	563	day-bright
247	ring-bone,	586	meane-while.
254	muſk-balls	633	holi-day
370	𝔊ommon-wealth		working-day
373	raw-milke,	678	𝔏ute-ſtrings,
	ſower-milke,	684	𝔏ute-ſtrings
	ſweete-milk,	693	after-noone,
	butter-milke,		

also anomalously:

366–7	there-|foꝛe	661–2	neigh-|bour,
612–3	ſure-|ly		

Lastly, the following alterations should be made:

801 *for* hiding *read* biding   1004 *for* ſall *read* ſall

also there should be no leads above or below 1969, and no period at the end of 2312. 'Sc. *viii*' should be opposite 951.

xxxiii

FACSIMILES

A

Looking Glaſse for

LONDON AND
England.

Made by *Thomas Lodge* Gentleman, and
Robert Greene.

In Artibus Magiſter.

LONDON
Printed by Thomas Creede, and are to be
ſold by William Barley, at his ſhop
in Gracious ſtreete.
1 5 9 4.

A LOOKING GLASSE FOR
London and England.

Enters *Rasin* King of *Niniuie*, with three Kings of *Cicilia*, *Creete*, and *Paphlagonia*, from the ouerthrow of *Ieroboam*, King of *Ierusalem*.

O pace ye on tryumphant warriours,
Make Venus Lemmon armd in al his pomp,
Bash at the brightnesse of your hardy lookes,
For you the Viceroyes and the Caualires,
That wait on Rasins royall mightinesse:
Boast pettie kings, and glory in your fates,
That stars haue made your fortunes clime so (high,
To giue attend on Rasins excellence.

Am I not he that rules great Niniuie,
Rounded with Lycas siluer flowing streams,
Whose Citie large Diametri containes,
Euen three daies tournies length from wall to wall,
Two hundreth gates carued out of burnisht brasse,
As glorious as the portoyle of the Sunne,
And for to decke heauens battlements with pride,
Sir hundreth Towers that toplesse touch the cloudes:
This Citie is the sootestoole of your King,
A hundreth Lords do honour at my feete,
My scepter straineth both the poralels,
And now to t'enlarge the highnesse of my power,
I haue made Iudeas Monarch flee the field,
And beat proud Ieroboam from his holds,
Winning from Cades to Samaria,

A 3   Great

1594. Beginning of Text (Hunt.)

and England.

And slept secure, when we for succour praide :
Him I awoke, and said why slumberest thou?
Arise and pray, and call vpon thy God,
He will perhaps in pitie looke on vs.
Then cast we lots to know by whose amisse
Our mischiefe come, according to the guise,
And loe the lot did vnto Ionas fall,
The Israelite of whom I told you last,
Then question we his Country and his name,
Who answered vs, I am an Hebrue borne,
Who feare the Lord of heauen, who made the sea,
And fled from him for which we all are plagu'd,
So to asswage the furie of my God,
Take me and cast my carkasse in the sea,
Then shall this stormy winde and billow cease.
The heauens they know, the Hebrues God can tell,
How loth we were to execute his will:
But when no Oares nor labour might suffice,
We heaued the haplesse Ionas ouer-boord.
So ceast the storme, and calmed all the sea,
And we by strength of oares recouered shoare.
Gouer. A wonderous chance of mighty consequence.
Mer. Ah honored be the God that wrought the same,
For we haue vowd, that saw his wonderous workes,
To cast away prophaned Paganisme,
And count the Hebrues God the onely God.
To him this offering of the purest gold,
This mirrhe and Cassia freely I do yeld.
M. And on his altars perfume these Turkie clothes,
This gassampine and gold ile sacrifice.
Sailer. To him my heart and thoughts I will addict,
Then suffer vs most mightie Gouernour,
Within your Temples to do sacrifice.
Gouer. You men of Tharsus follow me,
Who sacrifice vnto the God of heauen,
And welcome friends to Ioppais Gouernor.   *Exeunt* a sacrifice.
                                        Oseas.

F 3

1594. A PAGE OF TEXT (HUNT.)

Ionas Wend on in peace, and prosecute this course,
You Ilanders on whom the milder aire
Doth sweetly breath the balme of kinde incre. se:
Whose lands are fatned with the deaw of heauen,
And made more fruitfull then Actean plaines.
You whom delitious pleasures dandle soft:
Whose eyes are blinded with securitie,
Unmaske your selues, cast error cleane aside.
O London, mayden of the mistresse Ile,
Wrapt in the foldes and swathing cloutes of shame:
In thee moe sinnes then Niniuie containes,
Contempt of God, dispight of reuerend age.
Neglect of law, desire to wrong the poore:
Corruption, whordome, drunkennesse, and pride.
Swolne are thy browes with impudence and shame.
O proud adulterous glorie of the West,
Thy neighbors burns, yet doest thou feare no fire.
Thy Preachers crie, yet doest thou stop thine eares.
The larum rings, yet sleepest thou secure.
London awake, for feare the Lord do frowne,
I set a looking Glasse before thine eyes.
O turne, O turne, with weeping to the Lord,
And thinke the praiers and vertues of thy Queene,
Defers the plague which otherwise would fall.
Repent O London, least for thine offence,
Thy shepheard faile, whom mightie God preserue,
That she may bide the pillar of his Church,
Against the stormes of Romish Antichrist:
The hand of mercy ouershead her head,
And let all faithfull subiects say, Amen.

FINIS.

1594. END OF TEXT ON I4ᵛ (HUNT.)

A
LOOKING
Glaſſe, for London
and Englande.

Made by Thomas Lodge
Gentleman, and *Robert Greene*.

In Artibus Magiſter.

LONDON
Printed by Thomas Creede, and are to be ſolde
by William Barley, at his ſhop in
Gratious ſtreete.
1598.

A Looking Glaſſe, For
London and England.

Enters *Raſni* king of *Niniue*, with three kings of *Cicilia*, *Creet*, and *Paphlagonia*, from the ouerthrow of *Ieroboam*, King of *Ieruſalem*.

Ô pace ye on triumphant warriours,
Make Venus Lemnô armd in al his pomp,
Baſh at the brightneſſe of your hardy lookes,
For you the Viceroyes and the Caualires,
That wait on Raſnies royall mightineſſe :
Boaſt pettie kings, and glorie in your fates,
That ſtars haue made your fortuns clime ſo (high,
To giue attend on Raſnies excellency.

Am I not he that rules great Niniuie,
Rounded with Lycas ſiluer flowing ſtreames,
Whoſe Citie large Diametri containes,
Euen thrêe daies iournies length from wall to wall,
Two hundreth gates carued out of burniſht braſſe,
As glorious as the portoyle of the Sunne,
And for to decke heauens battlements with pride,
Sir hundreth Towers that topleſſe touch the cloudes :
This Citie is the footeſtoole of your king,
A hundreth Lords do honour at my fête,
My ſcepter ſtraineth both the poralels,
And now to t'enlarge the highneſſe of my power,
I haue made Iudeas Monarch flæ the field,
And beat proud Ieroboam from his holds,
Winning from Cades to Samaria,

A 3

Great

1598. BEGINNING OF TEXT (B.M.)

A LOOKING

Glaſſe, for London
and Englande.

Made by Thomas Lodge
Gentleman, and *Robert Greene*.

In Artibus Magiſter.

LONDON
Printed by Thomas Creede, for Thomas Pavier, and
are to be ſold at his ſhop in Cornhill, neare the
Exchange, at the Signe of the Cat and
Parots. 1602.

A
LOOK.ING
GLASSE FOR.

London and England.

MADE

By *Thomas Lodge* Gentleman, and
Robert Greene.

In Artibus Magifter.

LONDON,
Imprinted by *Barnard Alſop*, and are to be ſold at
his houſe within Gartar place in Barbican.
1 6 1 7.

A Looking glasse, for $\frac{d}{q}$
london and England.

Enter rafni King of Niniuie with three Kings of Cicilia, Creet
and Parblagonia, from the ouerthrow of Ieroboham, King
of Ierufalam.

rafni.

    SO pace ye on tryumphant warriours,
    Vake Venus Lemmon armd in all his powpe,
    Wash at the brightnesse of your hardie lookes,
    For the Ulceroyes and the Caualiers,
That wait on rafnies royall mightinesse:
Boast pettie Kings, and glorie in your Fates,
that starres haue made your fortunes climbe so high,
to giue attend on rafnies excellencie.
am I not he that rules great Niniuie,
Rounded with Lycas siluer flowing streames;
Whose Citie large Diametri containes,
Euen three daies iournies length from wall to wall,
two hundreth gates carued out of burnisht brasse,
As glorious as the portaile of the Sunne,
and for to decke heauens battlements with pride,
Sixe hundreth Towres that toplesse touch the cloudes;
This Cittie is the footestoole of our King.
A hundreth Lords do honour at my feete,
my scepter straineth both the parallels,
And now t'enlarg the highnes of my power,
I haue made Iudeas Monarch flie the field,
and beat proud Ieroboam from his holds,
Winning from Cades to Samaria

And scorne al eies, to see remelias eyes,
Nymphs, Eunucks, sing, for Mauors draweth nigh,
Hide me in closure, let him long to looke,
For were a Goddesse fairer then am I.
I'e scale the heauens to pul her from her place,
  They draw the curtaines, and Musicke plaies.
  alui. Beleeue me, who she say that she is the fairest,
I thinke my penny siluer by her leaue.

  Enter rasni with his Lords in pompe, who makes a ward a-
    bout him, with him the Magi in great pompe.
  ras. Magi for loue of rasni, by your art,
By Magicke frame an arbour out of hand,
For faire remelia to disport her in,
Meane while, I wil bethinke me on such a pomp. Exit.
The Magi with her rods beate the ground, and from vnder
    the same riseth a braue arbour, the king returneth in
        another sute while the Trumpets sound.
  rasni. Blest be ye man of art that grace me thus,
and blessed be this day where Himen hies,
To ioyne in vnion pride of heauen and earth.
  lightning and thunder wherwith remelia is strooken,
What wondrous threatning noise is this I heare,
What flashing lightnings trouble our delights?
When I draw neere remelias royal tent,
I waking, dreame of sorrow and mischap.
  rada. Dread not O king at ordinary chance,
These are but common exaltations,
Drawne from the earth, in substance hot and drie,
Or moist and thicke, or Meteors combust,
Matters and causes incident to time,
Enkindling in the firie Region first,
Cut, be not now a Romane Augurer,
Approach the Tent, looke on remelia.
  rasni. Thou hast confirmd my doubts kind radagon,
Now ope ye folds where Queene of fauour sits,
carrying a Net within he curlde locks,
                                    C   Within

for London and England.

Diuel. Come art thou readie?

Clowne. I am readie, and with this cudgell I will coniure thee.

Diuel. Oh hold thy hand, thou kilst, thou kilst me.

Clowne. Then may I count my selfe I thinke a tall man, that am able to kil a diuel: Now who dare deale with me in the Parish? or what wench in Niniuie will not loue me, when they say, there goes he that beat the diuel.

Enters Thrasibulus,

Thrasi. Loathed is the life that now inforc'd I lean,
But since necessitie will haue it so,
(Necessitie it doth commaund the Gods)
Through euery coast and corner now I prie,
To pilfer what I can to buy me meate.
Here haue I got a cloke not ouer old,
Which will afford some little sustenance,
Now wil I to the broking Usurer,
To make exchange of ware for ready coine:

Alcon. Wife bid the trumpets sound a prize, a prize, marke the posie, I cut this from a new married wife, by the helpe of a horne thumbe and a knife, sixe shillings four pence.

Samia. The better luck ours, but what haue we here, cast apparell? Come away man the Usurer is neare, this is dead ware, let it not bid on our hands.

Thrasi. Here are my partners in my pouertie,
Enforc'd to seeke their fortunes as I doo.
Alas that few men should prossesse the wealth,
And many soules be forc't to beg or steele.

Alcon. well met.

alcon. Fellow begger whither now?

Thrasi. To the Usurer to get gold on commoditie.

Alcon. And I to the same place to get bent for my villany, see where the old crust comes, let vs salute him. God speed sir, may a man abuse your patience vpon a pawne?

G 2   Vsu.

London and England.

Beare witnes God, of my unfained zeale.
Come holie man, as thou shalt counsel me,
My court and cittie shal reformed be.   *Exeunt.*

  Ion. Wend on in peace, and prosecute this course,
You Ilanders on whom the milder aire
Doth sweetly breathe the balme of kind increase:
Whole lands are fatned with the dewe of heauen,
and made more fruitful then acteon plains
You whom delitious pleasures dandle soft:
Who eies are blinded with securitie,
Unmaske your selues, cast error cleane aside,
O London, maiden of the mistresse Ile,
wrapt in the folds and swathing clouts of shame,
In thee more sinnes then Niniuie containes:
contempt of God, despight of reuerend age,
Neglect of law, desire to wrong the poore;
corruption, whordome, drunkenes, and pride,
Swolne are thy brows with impudence and shame.
O proud adulterous glorie of the west,
thy neighbors burnes, yet doest thou feare no fire.
thy Preachers crie, yet doest thou stop thine eares.
the larum rings yet slepest thou secure:
London awake for feare the Lord doth frowne,
I set a loking glasse before thine eies,
O turne, O turne with weeping to thy God,
and thinke the praiers and vertues of thy Quéene,
Defers the plague, which otherwise would fall
Repent O London, least for thine offence,
thy shepheard faile, whom mighty God preserue.
that she may bee the pillar of his church
against the stormes of Romish antichrist;
the hand of mercie ouershead his head,
and let al faithful subiects saie amen.

FINIS.

A
Looking Glaſe for

LONDON AND
England.

Made by *Thomas Lodge* Gentleman, and
Robert Greene.

In Artibus Magiſter.

LONDON
Printed by Thomas Creede, and are to be
ſold by William Barley, at his ſhop
in Gratious ſtreete.
1 5 9 4.

A LOOKING GLASSE FOR
London and England.

Enters *Rafin* King of *Niniuie*, with three Kings of *Cicilia*, *Creete*, *Sc. i*
and *Paphlagonia*, from the ouerthrow of *Ieroboam*, King of *Ie-*
rufalem.

So pace ye on tryumphant warriours,
Make Venus Lemmon armd in al his pomp,
Bath at the brightneſſe of your hardy lookes,
For you the Viceroyes and the Caualires,
That wait on Rafins royall mightineſſe:
Boaſt pettie kings, and glory in your fates,
That ſtars haue made your fortunes clime ſo 10
To giue attend on Rafins excellence.   (high,
Am I not he that rules great Niniuie,
Rounded with Lycas ſiluer flowing ſtreams,
Whoſe Citie large Diametri containes,
Euen three daies iournies length from wall to wall,
Two hundreth gates carued out of burniſht braſſe,
As glorious as the portoyle of the Sunne,
And for to decke heauens battlements with pride,
Six hundreth Towers that topleſſe touch the cloudes:
This Citie is the footeſtoole of your King,   20
A hundreth Lords do honour at my feete,
My ſcepter ſtraineth both the poralels,
And now to t'enlarge the highneſſe of my power,
I haue made Iudeas Monarch flee the field,
And beat proud Ieroboam from his holds,
Winning from Cades to Samaria,
A 3   Great

A looking Glaſſe for London

Great Iewries God that foilde ſtout Benhadab,
Could not rebate the ſtrength that Raſni brought,
For be he God in heauen, yet Uiceroyes know,
Raſni is God on earth and none but he.   30

   Cicilia. If louely ſhape, feature by natures ſkill,
Paſſing in beautie faire Endymions,
That Luna wrapt within her ſnowy breſts,
Or that ſweet boy that wrought bright Venus bane,
Transſoumde vnto a purple Hiacynth,
If beautie Nunpareile in excellence,
May make a King match with the Gods in gree,
Raſni is God on earth, and none but hee.

   Creet. If martial lookes wrapt in a cloud of wars
More fierce then Mars, lightneth fro his eyes   40
Sparkling reuenge and dyre diſparagement:
If doughtie deeds more haughtie then any done,
Seald with the ſmile of fortune and of fate,
Matchleſſe to manage Lance and Curteler.
If ſuch high actions grac'd with victories,
May make a King match with the Gods in gree,
Raſni is God on earth, and none but hee.

   Paphlag. If Pallas wealth.

   Raſni. Uiceroyes inough, peace Paphlagon no
See wheres my ſiſter faire Remilia,   (more,   50
Fairer then was the virgin Dania,
That waits on Venus with a golden ſhow,
She that hath ſtolne the wealth of Raſnes lookes,
And tide his thoughts within her louely lockes,
She that is lou'd, and loue vnto your King,
See where ſhe comes to gratulate my fame.

        Enters Radagon with Remilia, ſiſter to Raſni, Aluia
            wife to Paphlagon, and other Ladies, bring
                  a Globe ſeated in a ſhip.
   Remilia. Uictorious Monarch, ſecond vnto Ioue,   60
Mars vpon earth, and Neptune on the Seas,

                                                    Whoſe

Whose frowne stroyes all the Ocean with a calme,
Whose smile, drawes Flora to display her pride,
Whose eye holds wanton Venus at a gaze,
Rasni the Regent of great Niniuie,
For thou hast foyld proud Ieroboams force,
And like the mustering breath of Æolus,
That ouerturnes the pines of Libanon,
Hast scattered Iury and her vpstart groomes,
Winning from Cades to Samaria,   70
Remilia greets thee with a kinde salute,
And for a present to thy mightinesse,
Giues thee a Globe folded within a ship,
As King on earth and Lord of all the Seas,
With such a welcome vnto Nyniuie
As may thy sisters humble loue afford.
   Rasni. Sister. The title fits not thy degree,
A higher state of honour shall be thine,
The louely Trull that Mercury intrapt,
Within the curious pleasure of his tongue,   80
And she that basht the sun-god with her eyes,
Faire Semele the choyce of Venus maides,
Were not so beautious as Remelia.
Then sweeting, sister shall not serue the turne,
But Rasnes wife, his Lemmon and his loue.
Thou shalt like Iuno wed thy selfe to Ioue,
And fold me in the riches of thy faire,
Remilia shall be Rasnes Paramour.
For why if I be Mars for warlike deeds?
And thou bright Venus for thy cleare aspect,   90
Why should not from our loynes issue a sonne,
That might be Lord of royall soueraintie?
Of twentie worlds, if twentie worlds might be,
What saist Remilia, art thou Rasnes wife?
   Remilia. My heart doth swell with fauour of thy
The loue of Rasni maketh me as proud   (thoughts,
As Iuno when she wore heauens Diademe.

                                 Thy

Thy ſiſter boꝛne was foꝛ thy wife by loue,
Had I the riches nature locketh vp,
To decke her darling, beautie when ſhe ſmiles,   100
Raſin ſhould pꝛancke him in the pꝛide of all.

 Raſin. Remelias loue is farre moꝛe either pꝛiſde,
Then Ieroboams oꝛ the woꝛlds ſubdue,
Loꝛdings ile haue my weddings ſumptuous,
Made gloꝛious with the treaſures of the woꝛld,
Ile fetch from Albia ſhelues of Margarites,
And ſtrip the Indies of their Diamonds,
And Tyre ſhall yeeld me tribute of her gold,
To make Remelias wedding gloꝛious,
Ile ſend foꝛ all the Damoſell Queenes that liue   110
Within the reach of Raſins gouernment,
To wait as hand=maides on Remelia,
That her attendant traine may paſſe the troupe
That gloꝛied Venus at her wedding day.

 Creete. Oh my Loꝛd, not ſiſter to thy loue,
Tis inceſt and too fowle a fact foꝛ Kings,
Nature allowes no limits to ſuch luſt.   (Loꝛd,

 Rada. Pꝛeſumptuous Viceroy darſt thou check thy
Oꝛ twit him with the lawes that nature lowes,
Is not great Raſin aboue natures reach,   120
God vpon earth, and all his will is law.

 Creet. Oh flatter not, foꝛ hatefull is his choice,
And ſiſters loue will blemiſh all his woꝛth.

 Radag. Doth not the bꝛightneſſe of his maieſtie,
Shadow his deeds from being counted faults.

 Raſin. Well haſt thou anſwered within Radon,
I like thee foꝛ thy learned Sophiſtri,
But thou of Creet that countercheckſt thy King,
Packe hence in exile, Radagon the Crowne,
Be thee Vicegerent of his royaltie,   130
And faile me not in what my thoughts may pleaſe,
Foꝛ from a beggar haue I bꝛought thee vp,
And graceſt thee with the honour of a Crowne,

Ye

Ye quandam king, what feed ye on delaies?

    Creete. Better no king then Uiceroy vnder him
That hath no vertue to maintaine his Crowne.

    Rasni. Remilias, what faire dames be those that wait
Attendant on thy matchlesse royaltie?

    Remilia. Tis Aluia, the faire wife to the king of Paphlagonia.

    Rasni. Trust me she is faire thatt Paphlagon a Iewell,   140
To fold thee in so bright a sweetings armes.

    Rad. Like you her my Lord?

    Rasni. What if I do Radagon?

    Rada. Why the she is yours my Lord, for mariage
Makes no exception, where Rasni doth command.

    Paphla. Ill doest thou counsel him to fancy wiues.

    Rada. Wife or not wife, what so he likes is his.

    Rasni. Well answered Radagon thou art for me,
Feed thou mine humour, and be still a king.
Lords go in tryumph of my happie loues,   150
And for to feast vs after all our broyles,
Frolicke and reuell it in Niniuie.
Whatsoeuer befitteth your conceited thoughts,
Or good or ill, loue or not loue my boyes,
In loue or what may satisfie your lust,
Act it my Lords, for no man dare say no.

    Smith. *Denesum imperium Cum Ioue nunc teneo.*

                              Exeunt.

    Enters brought in by an Angell *Oseas* the Prophet, and set   Sc. ii
           downe ouer the Stage in a Throne.   160

    Angell. Amaze not man of God, if in the spirit
Th'art brought from Iewry vnto Niniuie,
So was Elias wrapt within a storme,
And set vpon mount Carnell by the Lord,
For thou hast preacht long to the stubborne Iewes,
Whose flintie hearts haue felt no sweet remorse,
But lightly baluing all the threats of God,
Haue still perseuerd in their wickednesse.

                     B   Loe

Loe J haue brought thee vnto Niniuie,
The rich and royall Citie of the world,   170
Pampred in wealth, and ouergrowne with pride,
As Sodome and Gomorrha full of ſin,
The Lord lookes downe, and cannot ſee one good,
Not one that couets to obey his will,
But wicked all, from Cradle to the Cruch.
Note then Oſeas all their greeuous ſinnes,
And ſee the wrath of God that paies reuenge.
And when the ripeneſſe of their ſin is full,
And thou haſt written all their wicked through,
Jle carry thee to Iewry backe againe,   180
And ſeate thee in the great Ieruſalem,
There ſhalt thou publiſh in her open ſtreetes,
That God ſends downe his hatefull wrath for ſin,
On ſuch as neuer heard his Prophets ſpeake,
Much more will he inflict a world of plagues,
On ſuch as heare the ſweetneſſe of his boice,
And yet obey not what his Prophets ſpeake,
Sit thee Oſeas pondring in the ſpirit,
The mightineſſe of theſe fond peoples ſinnes,
    Oſeas. The will of the Lord be done.   190

                                   Exit Angell.

           Enters the Clowne and his crew of Ruffians,   Sc. i.
                  to go to drinke.

Ruffian. Come on Smyth, thou ſhalt be one of the Crew, be=
           cauſe thou knowſt where the beſt Ale in the Town
           is.
Smith. Come on, in faith my colts J haue left my M. ſtriking of
           a heat, and ſtole away becauſe J would keep you com=
           pany.
Clowne. Why what ſhall we haue this paltrie Smith with   200
           vs?
                                       Smith.

Smith. Paltry Smith, why you in⟨
        you that you speak pettie tre⟨a
        trade?

Clowne. Why flaue I am a gentleman o⟨

Smith. A Gentleman good fir, I remember ⟨
your progenitors, your father bare office in our ⟨
man he was, and in great difcredit in the parifh, ⟨
ed two fquiers liuings on him, the one was on ⟨
and then he kept the towne ftage, and on ⟨   l   210
him the Sertens man, for he whipt dogs out of the ⟨
fir, your father, why fir mee=thinks I fee the Gen⟨t
proper youth, he was faith aged fome foure & ten, his b⟨
colour, halfe blacke halfe white, his nofe was in the ⟨h
gree of nofes, it was nofe Autem glorificam, fo fet wit⟨
that after his death it fhould haue bin nailed vp in Copp⟨e
hall for a monument: well fir, I was beholding to you⟨r
ther, for he was the firft man that euer inftructed me in ⟨the
fterie of a pot of Ale.

   2. Well faid Smith, that croft him ouer the thumbs.   220

Clowne. Uillaine were it not that we go to be merry, ⟨m
pier fhould prefently quit thy opprobrious termes.
O Peter, Peter, put vp thy fword I prithie heartily into thy fc⟨
bard, hold in your rapier, for though I haue not a long reach⟨
haue a fhort hitter. Nay then gentlemen ftay me, for my ch⟨o
begins to rife againft him, for marke the words a paltry S⟨m
Oh horrible fentence, thou haft in thefe words I will ftand ⟨t
libelled againft all the found horfes, whole horfes, fore hor⟨fe
Courfers, Curtalls, Iades, Cuts, Hackneies, and Mares, whe⟨
upon my friend, in their defence, I giue thee this curfe, fhalt n⟨   230
be worth a horfe of thine owne this feuen yeare.

   1. Clowne. I prithie Smith is your occupation fo excelle⟨n
A paltry Smith, why ile ftand to it, a Smith is Lord of the foure
elements, for our yron is made of the earth, our bellowes blow
out aire, our flore holdes fire, and our forge water. Nay fir, we
reade in the Chronicles, that there was a God of our occupa=
tion.

laſſ)e for London
) a Cuckold.
r) he cald your father couſin, paltry ſmith,
w)o2d thou haſt defaced their wo2ſhipfull occu= 240

A)s how?
) ſtand to it, that a Smith in his kinde is a Phi=
gi)on and a Barber. Fo2 let a Ho2ſe take a cold, o2
)ith the bots, and we ſtraight giue him a potion o2
h) phiſicall maner that he mends ſtraight, if
t)ward diſeaſes, as the ſpuing, ſplent, ring=bone,
l o)2 faſhion, o2 ſir a galled backe, we let him blood & clap
e)r to him with a peſtilence, that mends him with a ve=
g)eance, now if his mane grow out of o2der, and he haue 250
e)llious haires, we ſtraight to our ſheeres and trim him
w)hat cut it pleaſe vs, picke his eares and make him neat,
)y indeed ſir, we are ſlouings fo2 one thing, we neuer vſe
y) muſk=balls to waſh him with, and the reaſon is ſir, becauſe
)an woe without kiſſing.
C)lowne. Well ſirrha, leaue off theſe p2aiſes of a Smyth,
b)2ing vs to the beſt Ale in the Towne.
o)w ſir J haue a feate aboue all the Smythes in Niniuie, fo2 ſir
J) am a Philoſopher that can diſpute of the nature of Ale, fo2
a)rke you ſir, a pot of Ale conſiſts of foure parts, Imprimis the 260
l)e, the Toaſt, the Ginger, and the Nutmeg.
Clowne. Excellent.
h)e Ale is a reſto2atiue, b2ead is a binder, marke you ſir two ex=
c)ellent points in phiſicke, the Ginger, oh ware of that, the phi=
loſophers haue w2itten of the nature of ginger, tis expullſitiue
in two degrees, you ſhal here the ſentence of Galen, it wil make
a man belch, cough, and fart, and is a great comfo2t to the hart,
a p2oper poeſie J p2omiſe you, but now to the noble vertue of
the Nutmeg, it is ſaith one Ballad J think an Engliſh Roman
was the authour, an vnderlayer to the b2aines, fo2 when the 270
Ale giues a buffet to the head, oh the Nutmeg that keepes him
fo2 while in temper.
Thus you ſee the diſcription of the vertue of a pot of Ale, now ſir
to

to put my phisical precepts in practise (so
any further.

Clowne. VVhats the matter now?
Why seeing I haue prouided the Ale, who is (t
wenches, for masters take this of me, a cup (o
wench, why alasse tis like an egge without salt, (or a re
without mustard.   280
Lead vs to the Ale, weele haue wenches inough, I w(a

Oseas. Iniquitie seekes out companions still,
And mortall men are armed to do ill :
London looke on, this matter nips thee neere,
Leaue off thy ryot, pride and sumptuous cheere.
Spend lesse at boord, and spare not at the doore,
But aide the infant, and releeue the poore :
Else seeking mercy being mercilesse,
Thou be adiudged to endlesse heauinesse.

Enters the Vsurer, a yoong Gentleman, and   *Sc. iv*
a poore man.   291

Vsurer. Come on, I am euery day troubled with these needie
companions, what newes with you, what wind brings you hi=
ther.

Gent. Sir I hope how far soeuer you make it off, you remem=
ber too well for me, that this is the day wherin I should pay you
mony that I tooke vp of you alate in a commoditie.

Poore man. And sir, sirreuerence of your manhood and gente=
rie, I haue brought home such mony as you lent me.

Vsurer. You yoong Gentleman is my mony readie.   300

Gentle. Truly sir this time was so short, the commoditie so
bad, and the promise of friends so broken, that I could not prouide
it against the day, wherefore I am come to intreat you to stand
my friend and to fauour me with a longer time, and I wil make
you sufficient consideration.

Vsurer. Is the winde in that doore, if thou hast my mony so it
is, I will not defer a day, an houre, a minute, but take the forfeyt

B 3   of

) ſir conſider that my loſſe was great by the
k)e vp, you knowe ſir I boꝛrowed of you foꝛtie 310
) I had ten pounds in money, and thirty pounds
), which when I came to ſell againe, I could get
poundes) foꝛ them, ſo had I ſir but fifteene poundes foꝛ
) In conſideration of this ill bargaine, I pꝛay you ſir
m)onth longer.

ur)er. I anſwered thee afoꝛe not a minute, what haue I to
do how thy bargain pꝛoued, I haue thy hand ſet to my booke that
thou receiuedſt foꝛtie pounds of me in mony.

Gent. I ſir it was your deuiſe that, to colour the Statute, but
your conſcience knowes what I had. 320

Poore. Friend thou ſpeakeſt Hebꝛew to him when thou tal=
keſt to him of conſcience, foꝛ he hath as much conſcience about
the foꝛfeyt of an Obligation, as my blinde Mare God bleſſe her,
hath ouer a manger of Oates.

Gent. Then there is no fauour ſir?

Vſurer. Come to moꝛrow to mee, and ſee how I will vſe
thee.

Gent. No couetous Caterpillar, know, that I haue made ex=
treame ſhift rather then I would fall into the hands of ſuch a ra=
uening panthar, and therefoꝛe here is thy mony and deliuer me 330
the recogniſance of my lands.

Vſurer. What a ſpight is this, hath ſped of his Crownes, if
he had miſt but one halfe houre, what a goodly Farme had I got=
ten foꝛ foꝛtie pounds, well tis my curſed foꝛtune, Oh haue I no
ſhift to make him foꝛfeit his recogniſance.

Gent. Come ſir will you diſpatch and tell your mony.

Strikes 4 a clocke.

Vſurer. Stay, what is this a clocke foure, let me ſee, to be paid
betweē the houres of thꝛee and foure in the afternoone, this goes
right foꝛ me, you ſir, heare you not the clocke, and haue you not a 340
counterpaine of your Obligation, the houre is paſt, it was to be
paid betweene thꝛee and foure, and now the clocke hath ſtrooken
foure,

foure, I will receiue none, Ile stand to the forfeyt of the recog=
nisance.

Gent. Why sir, I hope you do but iest, why tis but foure, and
will you for a minute take forfeyt of my bond, if it were so sir,
I was here before foure.

Vsurer. Why didst thou not tender thy mony then? if I offer
thee iniury take the law of me, complaine to the Iudge, I will re=
ceiue no mony.   350

Poore. Well sir, I hope you will stand my good maister for
my Cow, I borrowed thirtie shillings on her, and for that I haue
paid you 18. pence a weeke, and for her meate you haue had her
milke, and I tell you sir, she giues a goodly soape: now sir here is
your mony.

Vsurer. Hang beggarly knaue, commest to me for a Cow, did
I not bind her bought and sold for a peny, and was not thy day to
haue paid yesterday, thou getst no Cow at my hand.

Poore. No Cow sir, alasse that word no Cow, goes as cold to
my heart as a draught of small drinke in a frostie morning.   No   360
Cow sir, why alasse, alasse, M. Vsurer, what shall become of me
my wife, and my poore childe?

Vsurer. Thou getst no Cow of me knaue, I cannot stand pra=
ting with you, I must be gone.

Poore. Nay but heare you M. Vsurer, no Cow, why sir heres
your thirtie shillings, I haue paid you 18. pence a weeke, & there=
fore there is reason I should haue my Cow.

Vsurer. What pratest thou, haue I not answered thee thy day
is broken?

Poore. Why sir alasse, my Cow is a Common=wealth to me,   370
for first sir, she allowes me, my wife and sonne, for to banket our
selues withal, Butter, Cheese, Whay, Curds, Creame, sod milk,
raw=milke, sower=milke, sweete=milk, and butter=milke, besides
sir, she saued me euery yeare a peny in Almanackes, for she was
as good to me as a Prognostication, if she had but set vp her tayle
and haue gallapt about the meade, my litle boy was able to say,
oh father there will be a storme, her verie taile was a Kalender
to me, & now to loose my cow, alas M. Vsurer take pittie vpõ me.

Vsurer.

Vſurer. J haue other matters to talke on, farwell fellowes.

Gent. Why but thou couetous churle, wilt thou not receiue 380 thy mony and deliuer me my recogniſance?

Vſurer. Jle deliuer thee none, if J haue wronged thee, ſeeke thy mends at the law.

Gent. And ſo J will inſatiable peſant.

Poore. And ſir, rather then J will put vp this word no Cow, J will laie my wiues beſt gowne to pawne, J tell you ſir, when the ſlaue vttered this word no Cow, it ſtrooke to my heart, for my wife ſhall neuer haue one ſo fit for her turne againe, for indeed ſir, ſhe is a woman that hath her twidling ſtrings broke.

Gent. What meaneſt thou by that fellow? 390

Poore. Marry ſir, ſirreuerence of your manhood, ſhe breakes winde behinde, and indeed ſir, when ſhe ſat milking of her Cow and let a fart, my other Cowes would ſtart at the noyſe, and kick downe the milke and away, but this Cow ſir the gentleſt Cow, my wife might blow whilſt ſhe burſt, and hauing ſuch good con=ditions, ſhall the Vſurer come vpon me with no Cow: Nay ſir, before J pocket vp this word no Cow, my wiues gowne goes to the Lawier, why alaſſe ſir tis as ill a word to me, as no Crowne to a King.

Gent. Well fellow, go with me, and ile helpe thee to a Law= 400 yer.

Poore. Marry and J will ſir: No Cow, well the world goes hard.   *Exeunt.*

Oſeas.

Oſeas. Where hatefull vſurie
Is counted husbandrie,
Where mercileſſe men rob the poore,
And the needie are thruſt out of doore.
Where gaine is held for conſcience,
And mens pleaſures is all on pence,   410
Where yong Gentlemen forfeit their lands,
Through riot, into the Vſurers hands:
Where pouertie is deſpiſde & pity baniſhed
And mercy indeed vtterly vaniſhed.

Where

and England.

Where men esteeme more of mony then of God,
Let that land looke to feele his wrathfull rod.
For there is no sin more odious in his sight,
Then where vsurie defraudes the poore of his right.
London take heed, these sinnes abound in thee:
The poore complaine, the widowes wronged bee.   420
The Gentlemen by subtiltie are spoilde,
The plough-men loose the crop for which they toild.
Sin raignes in thee ò London euery houre,
Repent and tempt not thus the heauenly power.

Enters Remilia, with a traine of Ladies   *Sc. v*
in all royaltie.

Remilia. **Faire Queenes, yet handmaids vnto** Rasnes **loue,**
Tell me, is not my state as glorious
As Iunoes **pomp, when tyred with heauens despoile,**
Clad in her vestments, spotted all with starres,   430
She croft the siluer path vnto her Ioue,
Is not Remilias **far more beautious,**
Richt with the pride of natures excellence?
Then Venus **in the brightest of her shine.**
My haires, surpasse they not Apollos **locks,**
Are not my Tresses curled with such art,
As loue delights to hide him in their faire?
Doth not mine eyne shine like the morning lampe
That tels Anrera **when her loue will come?**
Haue I not stolne the beautie of the heauens,   440
And plac'st it on the feature of my face?
Can any Goddesse make compare with me?
Or match her with the faire Remilia?

Aluida. **The beauties ỹ proud** Paris **saw fro** Troy
Mustring in Ida **for the golden ball,**
Were not so gorgious as Remilia.

Remilia. **I haue trickt my tramels vp with richest balme,**
And made my perfumes of the purest Myrre:
The pretious drugs that Aegypts **wealth affoords,**
        C   The

The coſtly paintings fetcht fro curious Tyre,   450
Haue mended in my face what nature miſt.
Am I not the earths wonder in my lookes?

   Alui. The wonder of the earth & pride of heauen.

   Remilia. Looke Aluida a haire ſtands not amiſſe,
For womens locks are tramels of conceit,
Which do intangle loue for all his wiles.

   Aluid. Madam, bnleſſe you coy it trick and trim,
And plaie the ciuill wanton ere you yeeld,
Smiting diſdaine of pleaſures with your tongue,
Patting your princely Raſni on the cheeke,   460
When he preſumes to kiſſe without conſent:
You marre the market, beautie nought auailes.
You muſt be proud, for pleaſures hardly got,
Are ſweete, if once attainde.

   Remilia. Faire Aluida,
Thy counſell makes Remilia paſſing wiſe.
Suppoſe that thou weart Raſnes mightineſſe,
And I Remilia Prince of excellence.

   Aluida. I would be maiſter then of loue and thee.

   Remil. Of loue and me. Proud & diſdainful king,   470
Dar'ſt thou preſume to touch a Deitie,
Before ſhe grace thee with a yeelding ſmile?

   Aluida. Tut my Remilia, be not thou ſo coy,
Say nay, and take it.

   Remilia. Careleſſe and bnkinde,
Talkes Raſni to Remilia in ſuch ſort
As if I did enioy a humane forme?
Looke on thy Loue, behold mine eyes diuine,
And dar'ſt thou twit me with a womans fault?
Ah Raſni thou art raſh to iudge of me,   480
I tell thee Flora oft hath wooed my lips,
To lend a Roſe to beautifie her ſpring,
The ſea-Nymphs fetch their lillies from my cheeks.
Then thou bnkind, and hereon would I weepe.

   Alui. And here would Aluida reſigne her charge,

For

For were I but in thought Th'aſſirian King,
I needs muſt quite thy teares, with kiſſes ſweete,
And craue a pardon with a friendly touch,
You know it Madam though I teach it not,
The touch I meane, you ſmile when as you think il.   490

    Remi. How am I pleaſ'd to hear thy pritty prate,
According to the humor of my minde?
Ah Nymphs, who fairer then Remilia?
The gentle winds haue wooed me with their ſighes,
The frowning aire hath cleerde when I did ſmile,
And when I tract vpon the tender graſſe,
Loue that makes warme the center of the earth,
Lift vp his creſt to kiſſe Remelias foote,
Iuno ſtill entertaines her amorous Ioue,
With new delights, for feare he looke on me,   500
The Phœnix feathers are become my Fanne,
For I am beauties Phœnix in this world.
Shut cloſe theſe Curtaines ſtraight and ſhadow me,
For feare Apollo ſpie me in his walkes,
And ſcorne all eyes, to ſee Remilias eyes.
Nymphes, Knancks, ſing, for Mauors draweth nigh,
Hide me in Cloſure, let him long to looke,
For were a Goddeſſe fairer then am I,
Ile ſcale the heauens to pull her from the place.

         They draw the Curtaines and Muſicke   510
             plaies.

    Aluida. Beleeue me, tho ſhe ſay that ſhe is faireſt,
I thinke my peny ſiluer by her leaue.

    Enter Raſni with his Lords in pomp, who make a
      ward about him, with him the Magi
         in great pompe.

    Raſni. Magi for loue of Raſni by your Art,
By Magicke frame an Arbour out of hand,
For faire Remilia to deſport her in.
Meane-while, I will bethinke me on further pomp.   520
                    Exit.

        C 2   The

The Magi with their rods beate the ground, and from vnder
the ſame riſeth a braue Arbour, the King retur-
neth in an other ſute while the Trum-
pettes ſounde.

Raſni. Bleſt be ye man of Art that grace me thus,
And bleſſed be this day where Himen hies,
To ioyne in vnion pride of heauen and earth.
                    Lightning and thunder vvherevvith Remilia
                    is ſtrooken.   530
What wondrous threatning noyſe is this I heare?
What flaſhing lightnings trouble our delights?
When I draw neare Remelias royall Tent,
I waking, dreame of ſorrow and miſhap.
    Rada. Dread not O King, at ordinary chance,
Theſe are but common exalations,
Drawne from the earth, in ſubſtance hote and drie,
Or moiſt and thicke, or Meteors combuſt,
Matters and cauſes incident to time,
Inkindled in the firie region firſt.   540
Tut be not now a Romane Angurer,
Approach the Tent, looke on Remelia.
    Raſni. Thou haſt confirmd my doubts kinde Radagon.
Now ope ye foldes where Queene of fauour ſits,
Carrying a Net within her curled locks,
Wherein the Graces are entangled oft:
Ope like th’imperiall gates where Phœbus ſits,
When as he meanes to wooe his Clitia.
Necternall Cares, ye blemiſhers of bliſſe,
Cloud not mine eyes whilſt I behold her face.   550
Remilia my delight, ſhe anſwereth not.
                    He dravves the Curtaines and findes her ſtroken
                    vvith Thunder, blacke.
How pale? as if bereau’d in fatall meedes,
The balmy breath hath left her boſome quite,

                                                              My

My Heſperus by cloudie death is blent,
Uillaines away, fetch Sirropes of the Inde,
Fetch Balſomo the kind preſerue of life,
Fetch wine of Greece, fetch oiles, fetch herbes, fetch all
To fetch her life, oꝛ J will faint and die.   560
       They bring in all theſe and offer, nought preuailes.
Herbes, Oyles of Inde, alaſſe there nought pꝛeuailes.
Shut are the day-bꝛight eyes, that made me ſee,
Lockt are the Jems of ioy in dens of death,
Yet triumph J on fate, and he on her.
Malicious miſtreſſe of inconſtancie,
Damd be thy name, that haſt obſcur'd my ioy,
Kings, Uiceroyes, Pꝛinces, reare a royall tombe
Foꝛ my Remilia, beare her from my ſight,
Whilſt J in teares, weepe foꝛ Remilia.   570
       They beare her out.
  Rada. What maketh Raſni moodie? Loſſe of one?
As if no moꝛe were left ſo faire as ſhe?
Behold a daintie minion foꝛ the nonce,
Faire Aluida the Paphlagonian Queene,
Wooe her, and leaue this weeping foꝛ the dead.
  Raſ. What wooe my ſubiects wife that honoꝛeth me?
  Rada. Tut Kings this meum tuum ſhould not know.
Js ſhe not faire? Js not her huſband hence?
Hold, take her at the hands of Radagon.   580
A pꝛittie peate to dꝛiue your mourne away.
  Raſni. She ſmiles on me, J ſee ſhe is mine owne.
Wilt thou be Raſnes royall Paramour?
  Rad. She bluſhing yeelds concent, make no diſpute:
The King is ſad, and muſt be gladded ſtraight.
Let Paphlagonian King go mourne meane-while.
       He thruſt the King out, and ſo they *Exeant.*
 Oſeas. Pride hath his iudgement, London looke about,
Tis not inough in ſhovv to be deuout,
A Furie novv from heauen to lands vnknovvne,   590
Hath made the Prophet ſpeake, not to his ovvne,
      C 3   Flie

A looking Glaffe for London

Flie wantons flie, this pride and vaine attire,
The feales to fet your tender hearts on fire.
Be faithfull in the promife you haue paft,
Elfe God will plague and punifh at the laft.
When luft is hid in fhroude of wretched life,
When craft doth dwell in bed of married wife.
Marke but the Prophets, we that fhortly fhowes,
After death exfpect for many woes.

Enters the poore man and the Gentlemau,
with their Lawier.

Gent. J need not fir difcourfe vnto you the dutie of Lawiers in tendering the right caufe of their Clients, no2 the confcience you are tied vnto by higher command. Therefo2e fuffife the Ufu=rer hath done me w2ong, you know the Cafe, and good fir, J haue ftrained my felfe to giue you your fees.

Lawier. Sir if J fhould any way neglect fo manifeft a truth, J were to be accufed of open periury, fo2 the cafe is euident.

Poore. And truly fir, fo2 my cafe, if you helpe me not fo2 my matter, why fir, J and my wife are quite bndone, J want my meafe of milke when J goe to my wo2ke, and my boy his b2ead and butter when he goes to fchoole, M. Lawier pitie me, fo2 fure=ly fir, J was faine to laie my wiues beft gowne to pawne fo2 your fees, when J lookt bpon it fir, and faw how hanfomly it was dawbed with ftatute lace, and what a faire mockado Cape it had, and then thought how hanfomely it became my wife, truly fir my heart is made of butter, it melts at the leaft perfecution, J fell on weeping, but when J thought on the wo2ds the Ufurer gaue me, no Cow: then fir, J would haue ftript her into her fmocke, but J would make him deliuer my Cow ere J had done, therefo2e good M. Lawier ftand my friend.

610

620

Lawier. Truft me father, J will do fo2 thee as much as fo2 my felfe.

Poore. Are you married fir?

Lawier. J marry am J father.

Poore. Then goods Benifon light on you & your good wife, and

and send her that she be neuer troubled with my wiues disease.

Lawier. Why whats thy wiues disease?

Poore. Truly sir, she hath two open faults, and one priuie
fault, sir the first is, she is too eloquēt for a poore man, and hath her 630
words of Art, for she will call me Rascall, Rogue, Runnagate,
Varlet, Vagabond, Slaue, Knaue. Why alasse sir, and these be
but holi-day tearmes, but if you heard her working-day words,
in faith sir they be ratlers like thunder sir, for after the dewe followes a storme, for then am I sure either to be well buffetted,
my face scratcht, or my head broken, and therefore good M. Lawyer on my knees I aske it, let me not go home again to my wife,
with this word, No Cow: for then shee will exercise her two
faults vpon me with all extremitie.

Lawier. Feare not man, but what is thy wiues priuy fault? 640

Poore. Truly sir, thats a thing of nothing, alasse she indeed
sirreuerence of your mastership, doth vse to breake winde in her
sleepe. Oh sir, here comes the Iudge, and the old Caitife the Vsurer.

      Enters the Iudge, the Vsurer, and his attendants.

Vsurer. Sir here is fortie angels for you, and if at any time
you want a hundreth pound or two, tis readie at your command,
or the feeding of three or foure fat bullocks: whereas these needie
slaues can reward with nothing but a cap and aknee, and therfore
I pray you sir fauour my case. 650

Iudge. Feare not sir, Ile do what I can for you.

Vsurer. What maister Lawier what make you here, mine
aduersary for these Clients?

Lawier. So it chanceth now sir.

Vsurer. I know you know the old Prouerbe, He is not wise,
that is not wise for himselfe. I would not be disgrast in this acti-
on, therefore here is twentie angels say nothing in the matter,
and what you say, say to no purpose, for the Iudge is my friend.

Lawier. Let me alone, Ile fit your purpose.

Iudge. Come, where are these fellowes that are the plain- 660
tifes, what can they say against this honest Citizen our neighbour, a man of good report amongst all men?

                           Poore.

Poore. Truly M. Judge, he is a man much fpoken off, marry euery mans cries are againft him, and efpecially we, and there-fore I thinke we haue brought our Lawier to touch him with as much law as will fetch his landes and my Cowe, with a peftilence.

Gent. Sir, I am the other plaintife and this is my Councel-lour, I befeech your honour be fauourable to me in equitie.

Iudge. Oh Signor Mizaldo, what can you fay in this Gentle-mans behalfe? 670

Lavvier. Faith fir as yet litle good, fir tell you your owne cafe to the Iudge, for I haue fo many matters in my head, that I haue almoft forgotten it.

Gent. Is the winde in that doore, why then my Lord thus, I tooke vp of this curfed Ufurer, for fo I may well tearme him, a commoditie of fortie poundes, whereof I receiued ten pounde in mony, & thirtie pound in Lute-ftrings, whereof I could by great friendfhip make but fiue pounds: for the affurance of this badde commoditie, I bound him my land in recognifance, I came at my 680 day and tendred him his mony and he would not take it, for the redreffe of my open wrong, I craue but iuftice.

Iudge. What fay you to this fir?

Vfurer. That firft he had no Lute-ftrings of me, for looke you fir, I haue his owne hand to my booke for y̆ receit of fortie pound.

Gent. That was fir, but a deuife of him to colour the Statute.

Iudge. Well he hath thine owne hand, and we can craue no more in law, but now fir, he faies his mony was tendred at the day and houre. 690

Vfurer. This is manifeft contrary fir, and on that I will de-pofe, for here is the obligation, to be paide betweene three & foure in the after-noone, and the Clocke ftrooke foure before he offered it, and the words be betweene three and foure, therefore to be ten-dred before foure.

Gent. Sir, I was there before foure, & he held me with brab-ling till the Clock ftrooke, and then for the breach of a minute he refufed my money, and keepe the recognifance of my land for fo

fmall

ſmall a triſtle: Good Signor Mizaldo ſpeak what is law, you haue your fee, you haue heard what the caſe is, and therefore do me iu= ſtice and right, I am a yoong Gentleman and ſpeake for my pa= trimony. 700

Lawier. Faith ſir, the Caſe is altered, you told me it before in an other maner, the law goes quite againſt you, and therfore you muſt pleade to the Iudge for fauour.

Gent. O execrable bribery.

Poore. Faith ſir Iudge, I pray you let me be the Gentlemans Counſellour, for I can ſay thus much in his defence, that the U= ſurers Clocke is the ſwifteſt Clock in all the Towne, tis ſir like a womans tongue, it goes euer halfe an houre before the time, 710 for when we were gone from him, other Clocks in the Towne ſtrooke foure.

Iudge. Hold thy prating fellow; and you yoong Gentleman, this is my ward, looke better another time both to your bargains and to the paiments, for I muſt giue flat ſentence againſt you, that for default of tendering the mony betweene the houres, you haue forfeited your recogniſance, and he to haue the land.

Gent. O inſpeakeable iniuſtice.

Poore. O monſtrous, miſerable, moth-eaten Iudge.

Iudge. Now you fellow, what haue you to ſay for your mat= 720 ter?

Poore. Maiſter Lawier, I laid my wiues gowne to pawne for your fees, I pray you to this geere.

Lawier. Alaſſe poore man, thy matter is out of my head, and therefore I pray thee tell it thy ſelfe.

Poore. I hold my Cap to a noble, that the Uſurer hath giuen him ſome gold, and he chawing it in his mouth, hath got ẙ tooth= ache that he cannot ſpeake.

Iudge. Well ſirrha, I muſt be ſhort, and therefore ſay on.

Poore. M. maiſter Iudge, I borrowed of this man thirtie ſhil= 730 lings, for which I left him in pawne my good Cow, the bargaine was, he ſhould haue eighteene pence a weeke and the Cows milk for vſurie: Now ſir, aſſoone as I had gotten the mony, I brought it him, and broke but a day, and for that he refuſed his mony and

D   keepes

keepes my Cow ſir.

Iudge. Why thou haſt giuen ſentence againſt thy ſelfe, for in breaking thy day thou haſt loſt thy Cow.

Poore. Maſter Lawier now for my ten ſhillings.

Lawier. Faith poore man, thy Caſe is ſo bad I ſhall but ſpeak againſt thee. 740

Poore. Twere good thē I ſhuld haue my ten ſhillings again.

Lawier. Tis my fee fellow for comming, wouldſt thou haue me come for nothing?

Poore. Why then am I like to goe home, not onely with no Cow, but no gowne, this geere goes hard.

Iudge. Well you haue heard what fauour I can ſhew you, I muſt do iuſtice, come M. Mizaldo and you ſir, go home with me to dinner.

Poore. Why but M. Iudge no Cow, & M. Lawier no gowne, Then muſt I cleane run out of the Towne. 750
How cheere you gentleman, you crie no lands too, the Iudge hath made you a knight for a gentleman, hath dubd you ſir Iohn lack=land.

Gent. O miſerable time wherein gold is aboue God.

Poore. Feare not man, I haue yet a fetch to get thy landes and my Cow againe, for I haue a ſonne in the Court that is ei=ther a king or a kings fellow, and to him will I go & complaine on the Iudge and the Uſurer both.

Gent. And I will go with thee and intreat him for my Caſe.

Poore. But how ſhall I go home to my wife, when I ſhall 760 haue nothing to ſay vnto her, but no Cow. Alaſſe ſir my wiues faults will fall vpon me.

Gent. Feare not, lets go, Ile quiet her ſhalt ſee.

Exeunt.

Oſeas. Flie Iudges flie, corruption in your Court,
The Iudge of truth, hath made your iudgement ſhort.
Looke ſo to iudge that at the latter day,
Ye be not iudg'd with thoſe that wend aſtray.
Who paſſerh iudgement for his priuate gaine,
He well may iudge, he is adiudg'd to paine. 770

Enters

Enters the Clowne and all his crew drunke. *Sc. vii*

Clowne. Farewell gentle Tapster, maisters as good Ale as euer was tapt, looke to your feete, for the Ale is strong, well farwell gentle Tapster.

1. Ruffian. Why sirrha slaue, by heauens maker, thinkest thou the wench loue thee best becaufe she laught on thee, giue me but such an other word, and I will throw the pot at thy head.

Clowne. Spill no drinke, spill no drinke, the Ale is good, Ile tel you what, Ale is Ale, & so Ile commend me to you with heartie commendations, farewell gentle Tapster. 780

2. Why wherfore peafant fcornst thou that the wench should loue me, looke but on her, & ile thrust my daggar in thy bofome.

1. Ruffian. Well sirrha well, thart as thart, and fo ile take

2. Why what am I? (thee

1. Why what thou wilt, a slaue.

2. Then take that villaine, and learne how thou vfe me another time.

1. Oh I am slaine.

2. Thats all one to me, I care not, now wil I in to my wench and call for a fresh pot. 790

Clown. Nay but heare ye, take me with ye, for the Ale is Ale, cut a fresh toast Tapster, fil me a pot here is mony, I am no beggar, Ile follow thee as long as the Ale lasts: a peftilence on the blocks for me, for I might haue had a fall, wel if we shal haue no Ale ile fit me downe, and fo farwell gentle Tapster.

Here he fals ouer the dead man.

Enters the King, Aluida, the King of Cilicia, and of Paphlagonia, with other attendant.

Rafni. What flaughtred wretch lies bleeding here his last?
So neare the royall pallaice of the King, 800
Search out if any one be hiding nie,
That can difcourfe the maner of his death,
Seate thee faire Aluida, the faire of faires,
Let not the otrict once offend thine eyes,

L. Heres one fits here a sleepe my Lord,

Rafni. Wake him and make enquiry of this thing.

D · 2 Lord.

Lord. Sirrha you, heareſt thou fellow?

Clowne. If you will fill a freſh pot heres a peny, or elſe fare=
    well gentle Tapſter.

Lord. He is drunke my Lord.   810

Raſni. Weele ſport with him that Aluida may laugh.

L. Sirrha thou fellow, thou muſt come to the King.

Clowne. I wil not do a ſtroke of worke to day, for the Ale is
good Ale, and you can aſke but a peny for a pot, no more by the ſta=
tute.

L. Villaine heres the King, thou muſt come to him.

Clown. The King come to an Ale-houſe, Tapſter, fil me three
pots, wheres the King, is this he? giue me your hand ſir, as good
Ale as euer was tapt, you ſhall drinke while your ſkin cracke.

Raſni. But heareſt thou fellow, who kild this man?   820

Clowne. Ile tell you ſir, if you did taſte of the Ale, all Niniuie hath not ſuch a cup of Ale, it ſloures in the cup ſir, by my troth
I ſpent eleuen pence beſide three raſes of ginger.

Raſni. Anſwer me knaue to my queſtion, how came this man
    ſlaine?

Clowne. Slain, why Ale is ſtrong Ale, tis hufcap, I warrant
you twill make a man well, Tapſter ho, for the King a cup of ale
and a freſh toaſt, heres two raſes more.

Aluida. Why good fellow the King talkes not of drinke, he
would haue thee tell him how this man came dead.   830

Clowne. Dead nay, I thinke I am aliue yet, and wil drink a
ful pot ere night, but here ye, if ye be the wench that fild vs drink,
why ſo do your office, & giue vs a freſh pot, or if you be the Tap=
ſters wife, why ſo, waſh the glaſſe cleane.

Aluida. He is ſo drunke my Lord, theres no talking with
    him.

Clowne. Drunke, nay then wench I am not drunke, thart a
ſhitten queane to call me drunke, I tell thee I am not drunke, I
am a Smith I.

             Enters the Smith, the Clownes maiſter.   840

Lord. Sir here comes one perhaps that can tell.

Smith. God ſaue you maſter.

                                Raſni.

and England.

Rafni. Smith canſt thou tell me how this man came dead?

Smith. May it pleaſe your highneſſe, my man here and a crue
of them went to the Ale-houſe, and came out ſo drunke that one
of them kild another, and now ſir, I am faine to leaue my ſhop
and come to fetch him home.

Rafni. Some of you carry away the dead bodie, drunken men
muſt haue their fits, and ſirrha Smith hence with thy man.

Smith. Sirrha you, riſe come go with me.   850

Clowne. If we ſhall haue a pot of Ale lets haue it, heres mony, hold Tapſter take my purſe.

Smith Come then with me, the pot ſtands full in the houſe.

Clowne. I am for you, lets go, thart an honeſt Tapſter, weele
drinke ſixe pots ere we part.

                                                    Exeunt.

Rafni. Beautious, more bright then beautie in mine eyes,
Tell me faire ſweeting, wants thou any thing?
Conteind within the threefold circle of the world,
That may make Aluida liue full content.   860

Aluida. Nothing my Lord, for all my thoughts are pleaſde,
When as mine eye ſurfets with Raſnes ſight.

        Enters the King of Paphlagonia, male-content.

Rafni. Looke how thy huſband haunts our royall Courts,
How ſtill his ſight breeds melancholy ſtormes,
Oh Aluida I am paſſion paſſionate,
And vext with wrath and anger to the death,
Mars when he held faire Venus on his knee,
And ſaw the limping Smith come from his forge,
Had not more deeper furrowes in his brow,   870
Then Rafni hath to ſee this Paphlagon.

Alui. Content thee ſweet, ile ſalue thy ſorow ſtraight,
Reſt but the eaſe of all thy thoughts on me,
And if I make not Rafni blyth againe,
Then ſay that womens fancies haue no ſhifts.

Paphla. Shamſt thou not Rafni though thou beeſt a King,
To ſhroude adultry in thy royall ſeate,
Art thou arch-ruler of great Niniuie,

                D 3   Who

Who ſhouldſt excell in vertue as in ſtate,
And wrongſt thy friend by keeping backe his wife,   880
Haue I not battail'd in thy troupes full oft,
Gainſt Aegypt, Iury, and proud Babylon,
Spending my blood to purchaſe thy renowne,
And is the guerdon of my chiualrie,
Ended in this abuſing of my wife,
Reſtore her me, or I will from thy Courts,
And make diſcourſe of thy adulterous deeds.
    Raſ. Why take her Paphlagon, exclaime not man,
For I do priſe mine honour more then loue.
Faire Aluida go with thy huſband home.   890
    Alui. How dare I go, ſham'd with ſo deep miſdeed,
Reuenge will broile within my huſbands breſt,
And when he hath me in the Court at home,
Then Aluida ſhall feele reuenge for all.
    Raſni. What ſaiſt thou king of Paphlagon to this?
Thou heareſt the doubt thy wife doth ſtand vpon,
If ſhe hath done amiſſe it is my fault,
I prithie pardon and forget all.
    Paphla. If that I meant not Raſni to forgiue,
And quite forget the follies that are paſt,   900
I would not vouch her preſence in my Courts,
But ſhe ſhall be my Queene, my loue, my life,
And Aluida vnto her Paphlagon
And lou'd, and more belou'd then before.
    Raſni. What ſaiſt thou Aluida to this?
    Alui. That will he ſweare it to my Lord the king,
And in a full carouſe of Greekiſh wine,
Drinke downe the malice of his deepe reuenge,
I will go home and loue him new againe.
    Raſni. What anſweres Paphlagon?   910
    Paphla. That what ſhe hath requeſted I wil do.
    Alui. Go damoſell fetch me that ſweete wine
That ſtands within thy Cloſet on the ſhelfe,
Powre it into a ſtanding bowle of gold,

But

and England.

But on thy life taſte not befoꝛe the king,
Make haſt, why is great Raſni melancholy thus?
If pꝛomiſe be not kept, hate all foꝛ me.
Here is the wine my Loꝛd, firſt make him ſweare.

 Paphla. By Niniuies great gods, and Niniuies great king,
My thoughts ſhall neuer be to wꝛong my wife,   920
And thereon heres a full carowſe to her.

 Alui. And thereon Raſni heres a kiſſe foꝛ thee.
Now maiſt thou freely fold thine Aluida.

 Paphla. Oh I am dead, obſtructions of my bꝛeath
The poiſon is of wondꝛous ſharpe effect,
Curſed be all adultrous queenes ſay I,
And curſing ſo pooꝛe Paphlagon doth die.

 Alui. Now haue I not ſalued the ſoꝛrowes of my
Haue I not rid ariuall of thy loues, (Loꝛd?
What ſaiſt thou Raſni to thy Paramour?   930

 Raſni. That foꝛ this deed ile decke my Aluida,
In Sendall and in coſtly Suſſapine,
Boꝛdꝛed with Pearle and India Diamond,
Ile cauſe great Eol perfume all his windes,
With richeſt myꝛre and curious Ambergreece,
Come louely minion, paragon foꝛ faire,
Come follow me ſweet goddeſſe of mine eye,
And taſte the pleaſures Raſni will pꝛouide. Exeunt.

 Oſeas. Where whordome raines, there murther followes faſt,
As falling leaues before the winter blaſt.   940
A wicked life trainde vp in endleſſe crime,
Hath no regard vnto the latter time.
When Letchers ſhall be puniſht for their luſt,
When Princes plagu'd becauſe they are vniuſt.
Foreſee in time the warning bell doth towle,
Subdue the fleſh, by praier to ſaue the ſoule.
London behold the cauſe of others wracke,
And ſee the ſword of iuſtice at thy backe.
Deferre not off to morrow is too late,
By night he comes perhaps to iudge thy ſtate.   950
       Enter

Enter Ionas Solus.

Ionas. From forth the depth of my impriſoned ſoule,   Sc. vii
Steale you my ſighes, teſtifie my paine,
Conuey on wings of mine immortall tone,
My zealous praiers, vnto the ſtarrie throne:
Ah mercifull and iuſt thou dreadfull God,
Where is thine arme to laie reuengefull ſtroakes
Upon the heads of our rebellious race?
Loe Iſraell once that flouriſht like the vine,   960
Is barraine laide, the beautifull encreaſe
Is wholly blent, and irreligious zeale
Incampeth there where vertue was inthroan'd
Ah-laſſe the while, the widow wants reliefe,
The fatherleſſe is wrongd by naked need,
Deuotion ſleepes in ſinders of Contempt,
Hypocriſie infects the holie Prieſt,
Aye me for this, woe me for theſe miſdeeds,
Alone I walke to thinke vpon the world,
And ſigh to ſee thy Prophets ſo contem'd: 970
Ah-laſſe contem'd by curſed Iſraell.
Yet Ionas reſt content, tis Iſraels ſinne
That cauſeth this, then muſe no more thereon,
But pray amends, and mend thy owne amiſſe.
An Angell appeareth to Ionas.
Angel. Amithais ſonne, I charge thee muſe no more,
(I am) hath power to pardon and correct,
To thee pertains to do the Lords command.
Go girt thy loines, and haſt thee quickly hence,
To Niniuie, that mightie Citie wend,
And ſay this meſſage from the Lord of hoaſts,   980
Preach vnto them thſe tidings from thy God.
Behold thy wickedneſſe hath tempted me,
And pierced through the ninefold orbes of heauen,
Repent, or elſe thy iudgement is at hand.

This

This said, the Angell vanisheth.

Ionas Proſtrate I lye before the Lord of hoſtes,
With humble eares intending his beheſt,
Ah honoured be Iehouahs great command,
Then Ionas muſt to Niniuie repaire,
Commanded as the Prophet of the Lord,   990
Great dangers on this iourny do awaight,
But dangers none where heauens direct the courſe,
What ſhould I deeme, I ſee, yea ſighing ſee,
How Iſraell ſinne, yet knowes the way of truth,
And thereby growes the by-word of the world,
How then ſhould God in iudgement be ſo ſtrict?
Gainſt thoſe who neuer heard or knew his power,
To threaten vtter ruine of them all:
Should I report this iudgement of my God,
I ſhould incite them more to follow ſinne,   1000
And publiſh to the world my countries blame,
It may not be, my conſcience tels me no.
Ah Ionas wilt thou proue rebellious then?
Conſider ere thou fall what errour is,
My minde miſgiues, to Ioppa will I flee,
And for a while to Tharſus ſhape my courſe,
Untill the Lord vnfret his angry browes.

Enter certaine Merchants of Tharſus, a Maiſter and ſome Sailers.

M. Come one braue merchants now the wind doth ſerue,   1010
And ſweetly blowes a gale at Weſt Southweſt.
Our yardes a croſſe, our anchors on the pike,
What ſhall we hence and take this merry gale?
    Mer. Sailers conuey our budgets ſtrait aboord,
And we will recompence your paines at laſt,
If once in ſafetie we may Tharſus ſee,
M. weele feaſt theſe merry mates and thee.
    M. Mean-while content your ſelues with ſilly cates,
Our beds are boordes, our feaſts are full of mirth,

                         E   We

We vfe no pompe, we are the Lords of fee,   1020
When Princes fwet in care, we fwincke of glee.
Orious fhoulders and the pointers ferue,
To be our load-ftars in the lingering night,
The beauties of Arcturus we behold,
And though the Sailer is no booke-man held,
He knowes more Art then euer booke-men read.
 Sailer. By heauens well faid, in honour of our trade,
Lets fee the proudeft fcholler ftir his courfe
Or fhift his tides as filly failers do,
Then wil we yeeld them praife, elfe neuer none.   1030
 Mer. Well fpoken fellow in thine owne behalfe,
But let vs hence, wind tarries none you wot,
And tide and time let flip is hardly got.
 M. March to the hauen merchants, I follow you.
 Ionas. Now doth occafion further my defires,
I finde companions fit to aide my flight,
Staie fir I pray, and heare a word or two.
 M. Say on good friend, but briefly if you pleafe,
My paffengers by this time are aboord.
 Ionas. Whether pretend you to imbarke your felues?   1040
 M. To Tharfus fir, and here in Ioppa hauen
Our fhip is preft and readie to depart.
 Ionas. May I haue paffage for my mony then?
 M. What not for mony? pay ten filuerlings,
You are a welcome gueft if fo you pleafe.
 Ionas. Hold take thy hire, I follow thee my friend.
 M. Where is your budget let me beare it fir.
 Ionas. To one in peace, who faile as I do now,
Put truft in him who fuccoureth euery want.
                                        Exeunt.   1050
 Ofe. When Prophets new infpirde, prefume to force
And tie the power of heauen to their conceits,
When feare, promotion, pride, or fimony,
Ambition, fubtill craft, their thoughts difguife,
Woe to the flocke whereas the fhepheards foule,

                                                    For

and England.

For lo the Lord at vnawares fhall plague
The careleffe guide, becaufe his flocks do ftray:
The axe alreadie to the tree is fet,
Beware to tempt the Lord ye men of art.

Enter Alcon, Thrafibulus, Samia,
Clefiphon a lad.

Clefi. Mother, come meat oz elfe I die foz want.

Samia. Ah litle boy how glad thy mother would
Supply thy wants but naked need denies:
Thy fathers flender poztion in this wozld,
By vfury and falfe deceit is loft,
No charitie within this Citie bides:
All foz themfelues, and none to helpe the poore.

Clefi. Father fhall Clefiphon haue no reliefe?

Alcon Faith my boy I muft be flat with thee, we muft feed vpon prouerbes now. As neceffitie hath no law, a churles feaft is
better then none at all, foz other remedies haue we none, except
thy brother Radagon helpe vs.

Samia. Is this thy flender care to helpe our childe?
Hath nature armde thee to no moze remozfe?
Ah cruell man, vnkind, and pittileffe,
Come Clefiphon my boy, ile beg foz thee.

Clefi. Oh how my mothers mourning moueth me?

Alcon. Nay you fhall paie mee intereft foz getting the boye
(wife) befoze you carry him hence. Ah-laffe woman what can Alcon do moze? Ile plucke the belly out of my heart foz thee fweete
Samia, be not fo wafpifh.

Samia. Ah filly man I know thy want is great,
And foolifh I to craue where nothing is.
Hafte Alcon hafte, make hafte vnto our fonne,
Who fince he is in fauour of the King,
May helpe this hapleffe Gentleman and vs.
Foz to regaine our goods from tyrants hands.

Thra. Haue patience Samia, waight your weale from heauen,
Tho Gods haue raifde your fonne I hope foz this,

1070

1080

1090

E .2   To

To ſuccour innocents in their diſtreſſe.

Enters Radagon, Solus.

Lo where he comes from the imperiall Court,
Go let vs proſtrate vs before his feete.

Alcon. Nay by my troth, ile neuer aſke my ſonne bleſſing, che
trow, cha taught him his leſſon to know his father, what ſonne
Radagon, yfaith boy how doeſt thee?

Rada. Villaine diſturbe me not, I cannot ſtay.

Alcon. Tut ſonne ile helpe you of that diſeaſe quickly, for I
can hold thee, aſke thy mother knaue what cunning I haue to eaſe 1100
a woman when a qualme of kindneſſe come too neare her ſto=
macke? Let me but claſpe mine armes about her bodie and ſaie
my praiers in her boſome, and ſhe ſhall be healed preſently.

Rada. Traitor vnto my Princely Maieſtie,
How dar'ſt thou laie thy hands vpon a King?

Samia. No Traitor Radagon, but true is he,
What hath promotion bleared thus thine eye,
To ſcorne thy father when he viſits thee?
Ah-laſſe my ſonne behold with ruthfull eyes,
Thy parents robd of all their worldly weale,   1110
By ſubtile meanes of Vſurie and guile,
The Iudges eares are deaffe and ſhut vp cloſe,
All mercie ſleepes, then be thou in theſe plundges
A patron to thy mother in her paines,
Behold thy brother almoſt dead for foode,
Oh ſuccour vs, that firſt did ſuccour thee.

Rada. What ſuccour me, falſe callet hence auant?
Old dotard pack, moue not my patience,
I know you not, Kings neuer looke ſo low.

Samia. You know vs not. Oh Radagon you know,   1120
That knowing vs, you know your parents then,
Thou knowſt this wombe firſt brought thee forth to light,
I know theſe paps did foſter thee my ſonne.

Alcon. And I know he hath had many a peece of bread & cheeſe
at my hands, as proud as he is, that know I.

Thracib. I waight no hope of ſuccours in this place,

Where

Where children hold their fathers in difgrace.

Rada. Dare you enforce the furrowes of reuenge,
Within the browes of royall Radagon?
Uillaine auant, hence beggers with your brats,   1130
Marſhall why whip you not theſe rogues away?
That thus diſturbe our royall Maieſtie.

Cleſiphon. Mother I ſee it is a wondrous thing,
From baſe eſtate for to become a King:
For why meethinke my brother in theſe fits,
Hath got a kingdome, and hath loſt his wits.

Rada. Yet more contempt before my royaltie?
Slaues fetch out tortures worſe then Titius plagues,
And teare their toongs from their blaſphemous heads.

Thraſi. Ile get me gone, tho woe begon with griefe,   1140
No hope remaines, come Alcon let vs wend.

Ra. Twere beſt you did, for feare you catch your bane.

Samia. Nay Traitor, I wil haunt thee to the death,
Ungratious ſonne, vntoward and peruerſe,
Ile fill the heauens with ecchoes of thy pride,
And ring in euery eare thy ſmall regard,
That doeſt deſpiſe thy parents in their wants,
And breathing forth my ſoule before thy feete,
My curſes ſtill ſhall haunt thy hatefull head,
And being dead, my ghoſt ſhall thee purſue.   1150

Enter Raſni King of Aſſiria, attended on by his
foothſayers and Kings.

Raſni. How now, what meane theſe outcries in our Court?
Where nought ſhould ſound but harmonies of heauen,
What maketh Radagon ſo paſſionate?

Samia. Juſtice O King, iuſtice againſt my ſonne.

Raſni. Thy ſonne : what ſonne?

Samia. This curſed Radagon.

Rada. Dread Monarch, this is but a lunacie,
Which griefe and want hath brought the woman to,   1160
What doth this paſſion hold you euerie Moone?

E 3   Samia

Samia. Oh polliticke in ſinne and wickedneſſe,
Too impudent for to delude thy Prince.
Oh Raſni this ſame wombe firſt brought him foorth.
This is his father, worne with care and age,
This is his brother, poore vnhappie lad,
And I his mother, though contemn'd by him,
With tedious toyle we got our litle good,
And brought him vp to ſchoole with mickle charge :
Lord how we ioy'd to ſee his towardneſſe,   1170
And to our ſelues we oft in ſilence ſaid,
This youth when we are old may ſuccour vs.
But now preferd and lifted vp by thee,
VVe quite deſtroyd by curſed vſurie,
He ſcorneth me, his father, and this childe.

Cleſi. He plaies the Serpent right, deſcrib'd in Æſopes tale,
That ſought the Foſters death that lately gaue him life.

Alcon. Nay and pleaſe your Maieſti-ſhip, for proofe he was my
childe, ſearch the pariſh booke, the Clarke wil ſweare it, his god=
fathers and godmothers can witneſſe it, it coſt me fortie pence in 1180
ale and cakes on the wiues at his chriſtning. Hence proud King,
thou ſhalt neuer more haue my bleſſing.

                                        He takes him apart.

Raſni. Say ſooth in ſecret Radagon,
Is this thy father ?
Rada. Mightie King he is,
I bluſhing, tell it to your Maieſtie.
Raſ. Why doſt thou then contemne him & his friends ?
Rada. Becauſe he is a baſe and abiect ſwaine,
My mother and her brat both beggarly,   1190
Unmeete to be allied vnto a King.
Should I that looke on Raſnes countenance,
And march amidſt his royall equipage,
Embaſe my ſelfe to ſpeake to ſuch as they ?
Twere impious ſo to impaire the loue
That mightie Raſni beares to Radagon.
I would your grace would quit them from your ſight

                                                    That

and England.

That dare prefume to looke on Ioues compare.

Rafni. I like thy pride, I praife thy pollicie,
Such fhould they be that wait vpon my Court.   1200
Let me alone to anfwere (Radagon.)
Villaines, feditious traitors as you be,
That fcandalize the honour of a King,
Depart my Court you ftales of impudence,
Vnleffe you would be parted from your limmes,
So bafe for to intitle father-hood,
To Rafnes friend, to Rafnes fauourite?

Rada. Hence begging fcold, hence caitiue clogd with
On paine of death reuifit not the Court.   (yeares,
VVas I conceiu'd by fuch a fcuruie trull,   1210
Or brought to light by fuch a lump of dirt:
Go Loffell trot it to the cart and fpade,
Thou art vnmeete to looke vpon a King,
Much leffe to be the father of a King.

Alcon. You may fee wife what a goodly peece of worke you
haue made, haue I tought you *Arfmetry*, as *additiori multiplica-*
rum, the rule of three, and all for the begetting of a boy, and to be
banifhed for my labour. O pittifull hearing. Come Clefiphon
follow me.

Clefi. Brother beware, I oft haue heard it told,   (old. 1220
That fonnes who do their fathers fcorne, fhall beg when they be
                                        Exet Alcon, Clefiphon.

Radagon. Hence baftard boy for feare you tafte the whip.

Samia. Oh all you heauens, and you eternall powers,
That fway the fword of iuftice in your hands,
(If mothers curfes for her fonnes contempt,
May fill the ballance of your furie full)
Powre downe the tempeft of your direfull plagues,
Vpon the head of curfed Radagon.

Vpon this praier fhe departeth, and a flame of fire appeareth   1230
        from beneath, and Radagon is fwallowed.

So you are iuft, now triumph Samia.   *Exet* Samia.
                                        Rafni

Raſni. What exorciſing charme, or hatefull hag,
Hath rauiſhed the pride of my delight?
What tortuous planets, or maleuolent
Conſpiring power, repining deſtenie
Hath made the concaue of the earth vncloſe,
And ſhut in ruptures louely Radagon?
If I be Lord-commander of the cloudes,
King of the earth, and Soueraigne of the ſeas,   1240
What daring Saturne from his fierie denne,
Doth dart theſe furious flames amidſt my Court?
I am not chiefe, there is more great then I,
What greater then Th'aſſirian Satrapos?
It may not be, and yet I feare there is,
That hath bereft me of my Radagon.
    Soothſaier. Monarch and Potentate of all our Prouinces,
Muſe not ſo much vpon this accident,
Which is indeed nothing miraculous,
The hill of Scicely, dread Soueraigne,   1250
Sometime on ſodaine doth euacuate,
Whole flakes of fire, and ſpues out from below
The ſmoakie brands that Vulueus bellowes driue,
Whether by windes incloſed in the earth,
Or fracture of the earth by riuers force,
Such chances as was this, are often ſeene,
Whole Cities ſuncke, whole Countries drowned quite,
Then muſe not at the loſſe of Radagon.
But frolicke with the dalliance of your loue.
Let cloathes of purple ſet with ſtuddes of gold,   1260
Embelliſhed with all the pride of earth,
Be ſpred for Aluida to ſit vpon.
Then thou like Mars courting the queene of loue,
Maiſt driue away this melancholy fit.
    Raſni. The proofe is good and philoſophicall,
And more, thy counſaile plauſible and ſweete.
Come Lords, though Raſni wants his Radagon,
Earth will repaie him many Radagons,

                                                      And

and England.

𝔄nd Aluida with pleasant lookes reuiue,
The heart that droupes for want of Radagon.

Exeunt.

Oseas. When difobedience raigneth in the childe,
And Princes eares by flattery be beguilde.
When lawes do paffe by fauour, not by truth,
When falfhood fwarmeth both in old and youth.
When gold is made a god to wrong the poore,
And charitie exilde from rich mens doore.
When men by wit do labour to difproue,
The plagues for finne, fent downe by God aboue.
Where great mens eares are ftop to good aduice,
And apt to heare thofe tales that feed their vice.
Woe to the land, for from the Eaft fhall rife,
A lambe of peace, the fcourge of vanities.
The iudge of truth, the patron of the iuft,
Who foone will laie prefumption in the duft.
And giue the humble poore their hearts defire,
And doome the worldlings to eternall fire.
Repent all you that heare, for feare of plagues,
O London, this and more doth fwarme in thee,
Repent, repent, for why the Lord doth fee.
With trembling pray, and mend what is amiffe,
The fwoord of iuftice drawne alreadie is.

1280

1290

Enter the Clowne and the Smiths wife.   *Sc. x*

Clowne. 𝔚𝔚hy but heare you mistresse, you know a womans
eies are like a paire of pattens fit to faue shooleather in sommer,
and to keepe away the cold in winter, so you may like your hus=
band with the one eye, becaufe you are married, and me with the
other, becaufe 𝔍 am your man. 𝔄lasse, alasse, think mistresse what
a thing loue is, why it is like to an oftry fagot, that once set on
fire, is as hardly quenched, as the bird Crocodill driuen out of
her neast.

Wife. Thy Adam cannot a woman winke but she must sleep,
and can she not loue but she must crie it out at the Crosse, know

𝔉   Adam,

1300

Adam, J loue thee as my felfe, now that we are together in fe=
cret.

Clown. Mif. thefe words of yours are like to a For taile placed
in a gentle womans Fanne, which as it is light, fo it giueth life.
Oh thefe words are as fweete as a lilly, wherupon offering a bo=
rachio of kiffes to your vnfeemly perfonage, J entertaine you vp=
on further acquaintance.   1310

Wife. Alaffe my hufband comes.

Clowne. Strike vp the drum, and fay no words but mum.

Smith. Sirrha you, and you hufwife, well taken togither, J
haue long fufpected you, and now J am glad J haue found you to=
gither.

Clowne. Truly fir, and J am glad that J may do you any way
pleafure, either in helping you or my miftreffe.

Smith. Boy here, and knaue you fhall know it ftraight, J wil
haue you both before the Magiftrate, and there haue you furely
punifhed.   1320

Clowne. Why then maifter you are iealous?

Smith. Jelous knaue, how can J be but iealous, to fee you euer
fo familiar togither? Thou art not only content to drinke away
my goods, but to abufe my wife.

Clowne. Two good quallities, drunkenneffe and leachery, but
maifter are you iealous?

Smith. J knaue and thou fhalt know it ere J paffe, for J will
befwindge thee while this roape will hold.

Wife. My good hufband abufe him not, for he neuer proffered
you any wrong,   1330

Smith. Nay whore, thy part fhall not be behinde.

Clowne. Why fuppofe maifter J haue offended you, is it law=
full for the maifter to beate the feruant for all offences?

Smith. J marry is it knaue.

Clowne. Then maifter wil J proue by logicke, that feeing all
finnes are to receiue correction, the maifter is to be corrected of
the man, and fir J pray you, what greater finne is, then iealoufie?
tis like a mad dog that for anger bites himfelfe. Therefore that
J may doe my dutie to you good maifter, and to make a white
                                                             fonne

ſonne of you, I will ſo beſwinge iealouſie out of you, as you ſhall 1340
loue me the better while you liue.

    Smith. What beate thy maiſter knaue?

    Clowne. What beat thy man knaue? and I maiſter, and dou=
ble beate you, becauſe you are a man of credite, and therfore haue
at you the faireſt for fortie pence.

    Smith. Alaſſe wife, help, helpe, my man kils me.

    Wife. Nay, euen as you haue baked ſo bꝛue, iealouſie muſt be
dꝛiuen out by extremities.

    Clowne. And that will I do, miſtreſſe.

    Smith. Hold thy hand Adam, and not only I forgiue and for= 1350
get all, but I will giue thee a good Farme to liue on.

    Clowne. Begone Peaſant, out of the compaſſe of my further
wꝛath, for I am a correctoꝛ of vice, and at night I wil bꝛing home
my miſtreſſe.

    Smith. Euen when you pleaſe good Adam.

    Clowne. When I pleaſe, marke the woꝛds, tis a leaſe paroll,
to haue and to hold, thou ſhalt be mine for euer, and ſo lets go to
the Ale-houſe.

Exeunt.

    Oſeas. Where ſeruants gainſt maiſters do rebell,   1360
The Common-weale may be accounted hell.
For if the feete the head ſhall hold in ſcorne,
The Cities ſtate will fall and be forlorne.
This error London, waiteth on thy ſtate,
Seruants amend, and maiſters leaue to hate.
Let loue abound, and vertue raigne in all,
So God will hold his hand that threatneth thrall.

    Enter the Merchants of Tharſus, the M. of the ſhip, ſome   *Sc. xi*
          Sailers, wet from ſea, with them the Gouer-
                nour of Ioppa.   1370

    Gouer. Iop. What ſtrange encounters met you on the ſea?
That thus your Barke is battered by the flouds,
And you returne thus ſea-wꝛackt as I ſee.

F   2   Mer.

Mer. Moſt mightie gouernoꝛ the chance is ſtrange,
The tidings full of wonder and amaȝe,
Which better then we, our M. can repoꝛt.

Gouer. M. diſcourſe vs all the accident.

M. The faire Triones with their glimmering light
Smil'd at the foote of cleare Rootes a raine,
And in the wꝛath diſtinguiſhing the houres,   1380
The Load-ſtarre of our courſe diſpearſt his cleare,
When to the ſeas with blithfull weſterne blaſts,
We ſaild amaine, and let the bowling flie:
Scarce had we gone ten leagues from ſight of land,
But lo an hoaſt of blacke and ſable cloudes,
Gan to eclips Lucinas ſiluer face,
And with a hurling noyſe from fooꝛth the South,
A guſt of winde did reare the billowes vp,
Then ſcantled we our ſailes with ſpeedie hands,
And tooke our dꝛablers from our bonnets ſtraight,   1390
And ſeuered our bonnets from the courſes,
Our topſailes vp, we truſſe our ſpꝛitſailes in,
But vainly ſtriue they that reſiſt the heauens.
Foꝛ loe the waues incence them moꝛe and moꝛe,
Mounting with hideous roarings from the depth,
Our Barke is battered by incountring ſtoꝛmes,
And welny ſtemd by bꝛeaking of the flouds,
The ſteers-man pale, and carefull holds his helme,
Wherein the truſt of life and ſafetie laie,
Till all at once (a moꝛtall tale to tell)   1400
Our ſailes were ſplit by Biſas bitter blaſt,
Our rudder bꝛoke and we bereft of hope,
There might you ſee with pale and gaſtly lookes,
The dead in thought, and dolefull merchants lifts,
Their eyes and hands vnto their Countries Gods,
The goods we caſt in bowels of the ſea,
A ſacrifice to ſwage pꝛoud Neptunes ire,
Onely alone a man of Iſraell,
A paſſenger, did vnder hatches lie,

And

And slept secure, when we for succour praide: 1410
Him I awooke, and said why slumberest thou?
Arise and pray, and call vpon thy God,
He will perhaps in pitie looke on vs.
Then cast we lots to know by whose amisse
Our mischiefe come, according to the guise,
And loe the lot did vnto Ionas fall,
The Israelite of whom I told you last,
Then question we his Country and his name,
Who answered vs, I am an Hebrue borne,
Who feare the Lord of heauen, who made the sea, 1420
And fled from him for which we all are plagu'd,
So to asswage the furie of my God,
Take me and cast my carkasse in the sea,
Then shall this stormy winde and billow cease.
The heauens they know, the Hebrues God can tell,
How loth we were to execute his will:
But when no Oares nor labour might suffice,
We heaued the haplesse Ionas ouer-boord.
So ceast the storme, and calmed all the sea,
And we by strength of oares recouered shoare. 1430

    Gouer. A wonderous chance of mighty consequence.

    Mer. Ah honored be the God that wrought the same,
For we haue vowd, that saw his wonderous workes,
To cast away prophaned Paganisme,
And count the Hebrues God the onely God.
To him this offering of the purest gold,
This mirrhe and Cassia freely I do yeeld.

    M. And on his altars perfume these Turkie clothes,
This gassampine and gold ile sacrifice.

    Sailer. To him my heart and thoughts I will addict, 1440
Then suffer vs most mightie Gouernour,
Within your Temples to do sacrifice.

    Gouer. You men of Tharsus follow me,
Who sacrifice vnto the God of heauen,
And welcome friends to Ioppais Gouernor.   *Exeunt* a sacrifice.
F 3   *Oseas.*

A looking Glaffe for London

Ofeas. If warned once, the Ethnicks thus repent,
And at the firft their errour do lament:
What fenfleffe beafts deuoured in their finne,
Are they whom long perfwations cannot winne.
Beware ye wefterne Cities where the word   1450
Is daily preached both at church and boord :
Where maieftie the Gofpell doth maintaine,
Where Preachers for your good, themfelues do paine.
To dally long, and ftill protract the time,
The Lord is iuft, and you but duft and flime :
Prefume not far, delaie not to amend,
Who fuffereth long, will punifh in the end.
Caft thy account ò London in this cafe,
Then iudge what caufe thou haft, to call for grace.   1459

Ionas the Prophet caft out of the Whales   *Sc. xi*
belly vpon the Stage.

Ionas. Loꝛd of the light, thou maker of the woꝛld,
Behold thy hands of mercy reares me vp,
Loe from the hidious bowels of this fiſh,
Thou haſt returnd me to the wiſhed aire,
Loe here apparant witneſſe of thy power,
The pꝛoud Leuiathan that ſcoures the ſeas,
And from his noſthꝛils ſhowꝛes out ſtoꝛmy flouds,
Whoſe backe reſiſts the tempeſt of the winde,
Whoſe pꝛeſence makes the ſcaly troopes to ſhake,   1470
With humble ſtreſſe of his bꝛoad opened chappes,
Hath lent me harbour in the raging flouds.
Thus though my ſin hath dꝛawne me down to death,
Thy mercy hath reſtoꝛed me to life.
Bow ye my knees, and you my baſhfull eyes,
Weepe ſo foꝛ griefe, as you to water would :
In trouble Loꝛd I called vnto thee,
Out of the belly of the deepeſt hell,
I cride, and thou didſt heare my voice O God :

Tis

and England.

Tis thou hadſt caſt me downe into the deepe, 1480
The ſeas and floods did compaſſe me about,
I thought I had bene caſt from out thy ſight,
The weeds were wrapt about my wretched head,
I went vnto the bottome of the hilles,
But thou O Lord my God haſt brought me vp.
On thee I thought when as my ſoule did faint,
My praiers did preaſe before thy mercy ſeate.
Then will I paie my vowes vnto the Lord,
For why ſaluation commeth from his throane.

        The Angell appeareth. 1490

  Angell. Ionas ariſe, get thee to Niniuie,
And preach to them the preachings that I bad:
Haſte thee to ſee the will of heauen perform'd.
                    Depart Angell.

  Ionas. Iehouah I am Prieſt to do thy will.
What coaſt is this, and where am I arriu'd?
Behold ſweete Licas ſtreaming in his boundes,
Bearing the walles of haughtie Niniuie,
Wheras three hundered towns do tempt the heauen.
Faire are thy walles pride of Aſſiria, 1500
But lo thy ſinnes haue pierced through the cloudes.
Here will I enter boldly, ſince I know
My God commands, whoſe power no power reſiſts.

                        Exet.

  Oſeas. You Prophets learne by Ionas how to liue,
Repent your ſinnes, whilſt he doth warning giue.
Who knowes his maiſters will and doth it not,
Shall ſuffer many ſtripes full well I wot.

     Enter Aluida in rich attire, with the King of   *Sc. xiii*
           Cilicia, her Ladies.   1510

  Aluida. Ladies go ſit you downe amidſt this bowre,
And let the Eunickes plaie you all a ſleepe:
Put garlands made of Roſes on your heads,

                        And

And plaie the wantons whilſt I talke a while.

Lady. Thou beautifull of all the woᵕld, we will.

Enter the bowers.

Aluid. King of Cilicia, kind and curtious,
Like to thy ſelfe, becauſe a louely King,
Come laie thee downe vpon thy miſtreſſe knee,
And I will ſing and talke of loue to thee. 1520

King Cili. Moſt gratious Paragon of excellence,
It fits not ſuch an abiect Pᵣince as I,
To talke with Raſnes Paramour and loue.

Al. To talke ſweet friend? who wold not talke with
Oh be not coy, art thou not only faire? (thee?
Come twine thine armes about this ſnow white neck,
A loue-neſt foᵣ the great Aſſirian King,
Bluſhing I tell thee faire, Cilician Pᵣince,
None but thy ſelfe can merit ſuch a grace.

K. Ci. Madam I hope you mean not foᵣ to mock me: 1530

Al. No king, faire king, my meaning is to yoke thee.
Heare me but ſing of loue, then by my ſighes,
My teares, my glauncing lookes, my changed cheare,
Thou ſhalt perceiue how I do hold thee deare.

K. Ci. Sing Madam if you pleaſe, but loue in ieſt,

Aluid. Nay, I will loue, and ſigh at euery reſt.

Song.

Beautie alaſſe where waſt thou borne?
Thus to hold thy ſelfe in ſcorne:
When as Beautie kiſt to wooe thee, 1540
Thou by Beautie doeſt vndo mee.

Heigho, deſpiſe me not.

I and thou in ſooth are one,
Fairer thou, I fairer none:
Wanton thou, and wilt thou wanton
Yeeld a cruell heart to plant on?
Do me right, and do me reaſon,
Crueltie is curſed treaſon.

Heigho I loue, heigho I loue,
Heigho, and yet he eies me not. King. 1550

and England.

King. Madam your song is passing passionate.

Alui. And wilt thou not then pitie my estate?

King. Aske loue of them who pitie may impart.

Alui. I aske of thee sweet, thou hast stole my hart.

King. Your loue is fixed on a greater King.

Alui. Tut womens loue, it is a sickle thing.

I loue my Rasni for my dignitie.

I loue Cilician King for his sweete eye.

I loue my Rasni since he rules the world.

But more I loue this kingly litle world.   Embrace him. 1560

How sweete he lookes? Oh were I Cinthias Pheere,

And thou Endimion, I should hold thee deere:

Thus should mine armes be spred about thy necke.

           Embrace his necke.

Thus would I kisse my loue at euery becke.

           Kisse.

Thus would I sigh to see thee sweetly sleepe:

And if thou wakest not soone, thus would I weepe.

And thus, and thus, and thus: thus much I loue thee.

           Kisse him.   1570

King. For all these vowes, beshrow me if I proue you:

My faith vnto my King shall not be fals'd.

Alui. Good Lord how men are coy when they are crau'd?

King. Madam behold our King approacheth nie.

Alui. Thou art Endimion, then no more, heigho for him I die.

           Faints. Point at the king of Cilicia.

           Enter Rasni, with his Kings and Lords.

What ailes the Center of my happinesse,

Whereon depends the heauen of my delight?

Thine eyes the motors to command my world,   1580

Thy hands the axier to maintaine my world.

Thy smiles, the prime and spring-tide of my world.

Thy frownes, the winter to afflict the world.

Thou Queene of me, I King of all the world.

Alui. Ah feeble eyes lift vp and looke on him, She riseth as out

Is Rasni here? then droupe no more poore hart, (of a traunce.

         G   Oh

Oh how I fainted when I wanted thee?

(Embrace him.

How faine am I, now I may looke on thee?
How glorious is my Raſni? how diuine?   1590
Eunukes play himmes, to praiſe his deitie:
He is my Ioue, and I his Iuno am.
   Raſni. Sun-bright, as is the eye of ſommers day,
When as he ſutes Spenori all in gold,
To wooe his Leda in a ſwanlike ſhape.
Seemely as Galbocia for thy white:
Roſe-coloured, lilly, louely, wanton, kinde,
Be thou the laborinth to tangle loue,
Whilſt I command the crowne from Venus creſt: 1600
And pull Onoris girdle from his loines,
Enchaſt with Carbunckles and Diamonds,
To beautifie faire Aluida my loue.
Play Eunukes, ſing in honour of her name,
Yet looke not ſlaues vpon her woing eyne,
For ſhe is faire Lucina to your king,
But fierce Meduſa to your baſer eie.
   Alui. What if I ſlept, where ſhould my pillow be?
   Raſni. Within my boſome Nimph, not on my knee.
Sleepe like the ſmiling puritie of heauen,
When mildeſt wind is loath to blend the peace,   1610
Meane-while thy balme ſhall from thy breath ariſe,
And while theſe cloſures of thy lampes be ſhut,
My ſoule may haue his peace from fancies warre.
This is my Morane, and I her Cephalus.
Wake not too ſoone ſweete Nimph, my loue is wonne:
Catnies why ſtaie your ſtraines, why tempt you me?

    Enter the Prieſt of the ſunne, vvith the miters on
       their heads, carrying fire in their hands.
Prieſt. All haile vnto Th'aſſirian deitie.
   Raſ. Prieſts why preſume you to diſturbe my peace?   1620
   Prieſt. Raſni, the deſtinies diſturbe thy peace.

                         Behold

Behold amidſt the addittes of our Gods,
Our mightie Gods the patrons of our warre.
The ghoſt of dead men howling walke about,
Crying Ve, Ve, wo to this Citie woe.
The ſtatutes of our Gods are throwne downe,
And ſtreames of blood our altars do diſtaine.

 Aluida. Ah-laſſe my Lord what tidings do I hear?
Shall I be ſlaine?

She ſtarteth.   1630

 Rafni. Who tempteth Aluida?
Go breake me vp the brazen doores of dreames,
And binde me curſed Morpheus in a chaine,
And fetter all the fancies of the night,
Becauſe they do diſturbe my Aluida.

A hand from out a cloud, threatneth a burning ſword.

 K. Cili. Behold dread Prince, a burning ſword from heauen,
Which by a threatning arme is brandiſhed.

 Rafni. What am I threatned then amidſt my throane?
Sages? you Magi? ſpeake: what meaneth this?   1640

 Sages. Theſe are but clammy exhalations,
Or retrograde, coniunctions of the ſtarres,
Or oppoſitions of the greater lights.
Or radiatrous finding matter fit,
That in the ſtarrie Spheare kindled be,
Matters betokening dangers to thy foes,
But peace and honour to my Lord the King.

 Rafni. Then frolicke Uiceroies, kings & potentates,
Driue all vaine fancies from your feeble mindes.
Prieſts go and pray, whilſt I prepare my feaſt,   1650
Where Aluida and I, in pearle and gold,
Will quaffe vnto our Nobles, richeſt wine,
In ſpight of fortune, fate, or deſtinie.

Exeunt.

 Oſeas. Woe to the traines of womens fooliſh luſt,
In wedlocke rights that yeeld but litle truſt.

G 2   That

That vow to one, yet common be to all,
Take warning wantons, pride will haue a fall.
Woe to the land where warnings profit nought,
Who ſay that nature, Gods decrees hath wrought.
VVho build one fate, and leaue the corner ſtone,
The God of Gods, ſweete Chriſt the onely one.
If ſuch eſcapes ô London raigne in thee:
Repent, for why each ſin ſhall puniſht bee.
Repent, amend, repent, the houre is nie,
Defer not time, who knowes when he ſhall die?

1660

Enters one clad in diuels attire alone. Sc. xi

Longer liues a merry man then a ſad, and becauſe I meane to make my ſelfe pleaſant this night, I haue put my ſelfe into this attire, to make a Clowne afraid that paſſeth this way: foꝛ of late 1670 there haue appeared many ſtrange apparitions, to the great fear and terroꝛ of the Citizens. Oh here my yoong maiſter comes.

Enters Adam and his miſtreſſe.

Adam. Feare not miſtreſſe, ile bꝛing you ſafe home, if my maiſter frowne, then will I ſtampe and ſtare, and if all be not well then, why then to moꝛrow moꝛne put out mine eyes cleane with foꝛtie pound.

VVife. Oh but Adam, I am afraid to walke ſo late becauſe of the ſpirits that appeare in the Citie.

Adam. What are you afraid of ſpirits, armde as I am, with 1680 Ale, and Nutmegs, turne me looſe to all the diuels in hell.

VVife. Alaſſe Adam, Adam, the diuell, the diuell.

Adam. The diuell miſtreſſe, flie you foꝛ your ſafegard, let me alone, the diuell and I will deale well inough, if he haue any honeſtie at all in him, Ile either win him with a ſmooth tale, oꝛ elſe with a toſte and a cup of Ale.

The Diuell ſings here.

Diuell. Oh, oh, oh, oh, faine would I bee,
If that my kingdome fulfilled I might ſee.
Oh, oh, oh, oh.

1690

Clowne. Surely this is a merry diuell, and I beleeue he is
one

one of Lucifers Minstrels, hath a sweete voice, now surely, surely, he may sing to a paire of Tongs and a Bag-pipe.

Diuell. Oh thou art he that I seeke for.

Clowne. Spritus santus, away from me satan, I haue nothing to do with thee.

Diuell. Oh villaine thou art mine.

Clowne. Nominus patrus, I blesse me from thee, and I coniure thee to tell me who thou art?

Diuell. I am the spirit of the dead man that was slaine in thy 1700 company when we were drunke togither at the Ale.

Clown. By my troth sir, I cry you mercy, your face is so chan-ged, that I had quite forgotten you, well maister diuell we haue tost ouer many a pot of Ale togither.

Diuell. And therefore must thou go with me to hell.

Clowne. I haue a pollicie to shift him, for I know he comes out of a hote place, and I know my selfe, the Smith and the diuel hath a drie tooth in his head, therefore will I leaue him a sleepe and runne my way.

Diuell. Come art thou readie.   1710

Clowne. Faith sir my old friend, and now goodman diuell, you know, you and I haue bene tossing many a good cup of Ale, your nose is growne verie rich, what say you, will you take a pot of Ale now at my hands, hell is like a Smiths forge full of water, and yet euer a thirst.

Diuell. No Ale villaine, spirits cannot drinke, come get vp on my backe, that I may carrie thee.

Clowne. You know I am a Smith sir, let me looke whether you be well shod or no, for if you want a shoe, a remoue, or the clinching of a naile, I am at your command.   1720

Diuell. Thou hast neuer a shoe fit for me.

Clowne. Why sir, we shooe horned beasts as well as you, Oh good Lord let me sit downe and laugh, hath neuer a clouen foote, a diuell quoth he, ile vse spritus santus nor nominus patrus no more to him, I warrant you Ile do more good vpon him with my cud-gell, now will I sit me downe and become Iustice of peace to the diuell.

G 3   Diuell.

Diuell. Come art thou readie?

Clowne. J am readie. And with this cudgell J will coniure thee.   1730

Diuell. Oh hold thy hand, thou kilst me, thou kilst me.

Clowne. Then may J count my felfe J thinke a tall man, that am able to kill a diuell. Now who dare deale with me in the pa= rifh, or what wench in Niniuie will not loue me, when they fay, there goes he that beate the diuell.

Enters Thrafibulus.   Sc. xv

Thrafi. Loathed is the life that now infor'd J leade,
But fince neceffitie will haue it fo,
(Neceffitie it doth command the Gods)
Through euerie coaft and corner now J prie,   1740
To pilfer what J can to buy me meate.
Here haue J got a cloake not ouer old,
Which will affoord fome litle fuftenance,
Now will J to the broaking Ufurer,
To make exchange of ware for readie coine.

Alcon. Wife bid the Trumpets found a prize, a prize, mark the pofie, J cut this from a new married wife, by the helpe of a horne thombe and a knife, fixe fhillings foure pence.

Samia. The better lucke ours, but what haue we here, caft ap= parell. Come away man, the Ufurer is neare, this is dead ware, 1750
let it not bide on our hands.

Thrafi. Here are my partners in my pouertie,
Infor'd to feeke their fortunes as J do.
Ah-laffe that fewe men fhould poffeffe the wealth,
And many foules be for'd to beg or fteale.
Alcon well met.

Alcon. Fellow begger whither now?

Thrafi. To the Ufurer to get gold on commoditie.

Alcon. And J to the fame place to get a bent for my billany,
fee where the olde cruft comes, let bs falute him, God fpeede fir 1760
may a man abufe your patience bpon a pawne.

Diuell.

and England.

Vſurer. Friend let me ſee it.

Alcon. *Ecce ſignum*, a faire doublet and hoſe, new bought out of the pilferers ſhop, a hanſome cloake.

Vſurer. How were they gotten?

Thraſi. How catch the fiſher-men fiſh? M. take them as you thinke them worth, we leaue all to your conſcience.

Vſurer. Honeſt men, toward men, good men, my friends, like to proue good members, vſe me, command me, I will maintaine your credits, there's mony, now ſpend not your time in idleneſſe, bring me commoditie I haue crownes for you, there is two ſhillings for thee, and ſix ſhillings for thee.

Alcon. A bargaine, now Samia haue at it for a new ſmocke, come let vs to the ſpring of the beſt liquor, whileſt this laſtes, tril-lill.

Vſurer. Good fellowes, propper fellowes, my companions, farwell, I haue a pot for you.

Samia. If he could ſpare it.

Enters to them Ionas.

Repent ye men of Niniuie, repent,   1780
The day of horror and of torment comes,
When greedie hearts ſhall glutted be with fire,
When as corruptions builde, ſhall be vnmaſkt,
When briberies ſhall be repaide with bane.
When whoredomes ſhall be recompenc'd in hell.
When riot ſhall with rigor be rewarded.
When as neglect of truth, contempt of God,
Diſdaine of poore men, fatherleſſe and ſicke,
Shall be rewarded with a bitter plague.
Repent ye men of Niniuie, repent.   1790
The Lord hath ſpoke, and I do crie it out.
There are as yet but fortie daies remaining,
And then ſhall Niniuie be ouerthrowne.
Repent ye men of Niniuie, repent.
There are as yet but fortie daies remaining,
And then ſhall Niniuie be ouerthrowne.   *Exet.*

Vſurer.

A Looking Glaffe for London

Vfur. Confuf'd in thought, oh whither fhall I wend? (*Exet.*
Thrafi. My confcience cries that I haue done amiffe. (*Exet.*
Alcon. Oh God of heauen, gainft thee haue I offended. (*Exet.*
Samia. Afham'd of my mifdeeds, where fhal I hide me? (*Exet.* 1800
Clefi. Father methinks this word repent is good,
He that punifh difobedience,
Doth hold a fcourge for euery priuie fault. (*Exet.*

Ofeas. Looke London, look, with inward eies behold,
What leffons the euents do here vnfold.
Sinne growne to pride, to mifery is thrall,
The warning bell is rung, beware to fall.
Ye worldly men whom wealth doth lift on hie,
Beware and feare, for worldly men muft die.
The time fhall come, where leaft fufpect remaines, 1810
The fword fhall light vpon the wifeft braines.
The head that deemes to ouer-top the skie,
Shall perifh in his humaine pollicie.
Lo I haue faid, when I haue faid the truth,
When will is law, when folly guideth youth.
When fhew of zeale is prankt in robes of zeale,
When Minifters powle the pride of common-weale?
When lavv is made a laborinth of ftrife,
When honour yeelds him friend to vvicked life.
When Princes heare by others eares their follie, 1820
When vfury is moft accounted holie.
If thefe fhall hap, as vvould to God they might not,
The plague is neare, I fpeake although I vvrite not.

Enters the Angell.

Angell. *Ofeas.*
Ofeas. Lord.
An. Now hath thine eies peruf'd thefe hainous fins,
Hatefull vnto the mightie Lord of hoftes,
The time is come, their finnes are waxen ripe,
And though the Lord forewarnes, yet they repent not: 1830
Cuftome

Cuſtome of ſinne hath hardned all their hearts,
Now comes reuenge armed with mightie plagues,
To puniſh all that liue in Niniuie,
For God is iuſt as he is mercifull,
And doubtleſſe plagues all ſuch as ſcorne repent,
Thou ſhalt not ſee the deſolation
That falles vnto theſe curſed Niniuites,
But ſhalt returne to great Ieruſalem,
And preach vnto the people of thy God,
What mightie plagues are incident to ſinne,   1840
Unleſſe repentance mittigate his ire :
Wrapt in the ſpirit as thou wert hither brought,
Ile ſeate thee in Iudeas prouinces,
Feare not Oſeas then to preach the word.
   Oſeas. The will of the Lord be done.

                         Oſeas taken away.

     Enters Raſni with his Viceroyes, Aluida and her   *Sc. xvi*
                 Ladies, to a banquet.
   Raſni. So Viceroyes you haue pleaſde me paſſing well,
Theſe curious cates are gratious in mine eye.   1850
But theſe Borachious of the richeſt wine,
Make me to thinke how blythſome we will be.
Seate thee faire Iuno in the royall throne,
And I will ſerue thee to ſee thy face,
That feeding on the beautie of thy lookes,
My ſtomacke and mine eyes may both be fild.
Come Lordings ſeate you, fellow mates at feaſt,
And frolicke wags, this is a day of glee,
This banquet is for brightſome Aluida.
Ile haue them ſkinck my ſtanding bowles with wine,   1860
And no man drinke, but quaffe a whole carouſe,
Unto the health of beautious Aluida.
For who ſo riſeth from this feaſt not drunke,
As I am Raſni Niniuies great King,
Shall die the death as traitor to my ſelfe,
              H   For

For that he ſcoines the health of Aluida.

K. Cili. That will I neuer do my L.
Therefore with fauour, foitune to your grace,
Carowſe vnto the health of Aluida.

Raſni. Gramercy Loiding, here I take thy pledge.   1870
And Creete to thee a bowle of Greekiſh wine,
Here to the health of Aluida.

Creete. Let come my Loid, Jack ſcincker fil it full,
A pledge vnto the health of heauenly Aluida.

Raſni. Uaſſals attendant on our royall feaſts,
Diinke you I ſay vnto my louers health,
Let none that is in Raſnes royall Court,
Go this night ſafe and ſober to his bed.

Enters the Clowne.

Clowne. This way he is, and here will I ſpeake with him.   1880
Lord. Fellow, whither pieſſeſt thou?
Clowne. I pieſſe no bodie ſir, I am going to ſpeake with a
friend of mine.
Lord. Why ſlaue, here is none but the King and his Uice=
ropes.
Clowne. The King, marry ſir he is the man I would ſpeake
withall.
Lord. Why calſt him a friend of thine?
Clowne. I marry do I ſir, foi if he be not my friend, ile make
him my friend ere he and I paſſe.   1890
Lord. Away vaſſaile be gone, thou ſpeake vnto the King.
Clowne. I marry will I ſir, and if he were a king of beluet, I
will talke to him.
Raſni. Whats the matter there, what noyce is that?
Clowne. A boone my Liege, a boone my Liege.
Raſni. What is it that great Raſni will not graunt
This day, vnto the meaneſt of his land?
In honour of his beautious Aluida?
Come hither ſwaine, what is it that thou craueſt?
Clowne. Faith ſir nothing, but to ſpeake a fewe ſentences to 1900
your woiſhip.

Raſni

Rafni, Say, what is it?

Clown. I am sure sir you haue heard of the spirits that walke in the Citie here.

Rafni. I, what of that?

Clown. Truly sir, I haue an oration to tel you of one of them, and this it is.

Alui. Why goest not forward with thy tale?

Clowne. Faith mistrelle, I feele an imperfection in my voyce, a difeafe that often troubles me, but alalle eafily mended, a cup of Ale, or a cup of wine, will ferue the turne. 1910

Alui. Fill him a bowle, and let him want no drinke.

Clown. Oh what a pretious word was that, and let him want no drinke. Well sir, now ile tel you foorth my tale: Sir as I was comming alongst the port ryuale of Niniuie, there appeared to me a great diuell, and as hard fauoured a diuell as euer I faw: nay sir, he was a cuckoldly diuell, for he had hornes on his head. This diuell, marke you now, presseth vpon me, and sir indeed, I charged him with my pike staffe, but when y would not ferue, I came vpon him with *fprytus fantus*, why it had bene able to haue 1920 put Lucifer out of his wits, when I faw my charme would not ferue, I was in fuch a perplexitie, that fixe peny-worth of Juni-per would not haue made the place fweete againe.

Alui. Why fellow weart thou fo afraid?

Clowne. Oh mistrelle had you bene there and feene, his verie fight had made you shift a cleane fmocke, I promife you though I were a man and counted a tall fellow, yet my Landrelle calde me flouenly knaue the next day.

Rafni. A pleafaunt flaue, forward sirrha, on with thy tale. 1930

Clowne. Faith sir, but I remember a word that my mistrelle your bed-fellow fpoake.

Rafni. What was that fellow?

Clowne. Oh sir, a word of comfort, a pretious word: and let him want no drinke.

Rafni. Her word is lawe: and thou shalt want no drinke.

Clowne.

Clowne. Then ſir, this diuell came vpon me and would not
be perſwaded but he would needs carry me to hell, I proffered
him a cup of Ale, thinking becauſe he came out of ſo hotte a place   1940
that he was thirſtie, but the diuell was not drie, and therfore the
more ſorie was I, well, there was no remedie but I muſt with
him to hell, and at laſt I caſt mine eye aſide, if you knew what I
ſpied you would laugh, ſir I lookt from top to toe, and he had no
clouen feete. Then I ruffled vp my haire, and ſet my cap on the
one ſide, & ſir grew to be a Iuſtice of peace to the diuel. At laſt in
a great fume, as I am very cholloricke, and ſometime ſo hotte in
my faſtin fumes that no man can abide within twentie yards of
me, I ſtart vp, and ſo bombaſted the diuell, that ſir he cried out,
and ranne away.   1950

Alui. This pleaſant knaue hath made me laugh my fill.
Raſni, now Aluida begins her quaffe,
And drinkes a full carouſe vnto her King.

Raſni. A pledge my loue, as hardie as great Ioue,
Drunke, when his Iuno heau'd a bowle to him.
Frolicke my Lord, let all the ſtanderds walke.
Ply it till euery man hath tane his load.
How now ſirrha, how cheere, we haue no words of you?

Clown. Truly ſir, I was in a broune ſtudy about my miſtreſſe.
Alui. About me for what?   1960

Clowne. Truly miſtreſſe, to thinke what a golden ſentence
you did ſpeake : all the philoſophers in the world could not haue
ſaid more : what come let him want no drinke. Oh wiſe ſpeech.

Alui. Uillaines why ſkinck you not vnto this fellow?
He makes me blyth and merry in my thoughts.
Heard you not that the King hath giuen command,
That all be drunke this day within his Court,
In quaffing to the health of Aluida?

Enters Ionas.

Ionas. Repent, repent, ye men of Niniuie repent.   1970
The Lord hath ſpoken, and I do crie it out,
There are as yet but fortie daies remaining,
And then ſhall Niniuie be ouerthrowne.

                                                          Repent

Repent ye men of Niniuie, repent.

Rasni. What fellow is this, that thus disturbes our feasts,
With outcries and alarams to repent.

Clowne. Oh sir, tis one goodman Ionas that is come from Ie-
richo, and surely I thinke he hath seene some spirit by the way,
and is fallen out of his wits, for he neuer leaues crying night nor
day, my maister heard him, and he shut vp his shop, gaue me my   1980
Indenture, and he and his wife do nothing but fast and pray.

Ionas. Repent ye men of Niniuie, repent.

Rasni. Come hither fellow, what art, & from whence commest
Ionas. Rasni, I am a Prophet of the Lord,   (thou?
Sent hither by the mightie God of hostes,
To cry destruction to the Niniuites,
O Niniuie thou harlot of the world,
I raise thy neighbours round about thy boundes,
To come and see thy filthinesse and sinne.
Thus saith the Lord, the mightie God of hoste,   1990
Your King loues chambering and wantonnesse,
Whoredome and murther do distaine his Court,
He fauoureth couetous and drunken men.
Behold therefore all like a strumpet foule,
Thou shalt be iudg'd and punisht for thy crime:
The foe shall pierce the gates with iron rampes,
The fire shall quite consume thee from aboue.
The houses shall be burnt, the Infants slaine.
And women shall behold their husbands die.
Thine eldest sister is Lamana.   2000
And Sodome on thy right hand seated is.
Repent ye men of Niniuie, repent.
The Lord hath spoke, and I do crie it out.
There are as yet but fortie daies remaining,
And then shall Niniuie be ouerthrowne.

                                   Exet offered.

Rasni. Staie Prophet, staie.
Ionas. Disturbe not him that sent me,
Let me performe the message of the Lord.   *Exet.*
                                                      Rasni.

Raſni. My ſoule is buried in the hell of thoughts.   2010
Ah Aluida, I looke on thee with ſhame.
My Lords on ſodeine fire their eyes on ground,
As if diſmayd to looke vpon the heauens.
Hence Magi, who haue flattered me in ſinne.
                                        Exet. His Sages.
Horror of minde, diſturbance of my ſoule,
Makes me agaſt, for Niniuies miſhap.
Lords ſee proclaim'd, yea ſee it ſtraight proclaim'd,
That man and beaſt, the woman and her childe,
For fortie daies in ſacke and aſhes faſt,   2020
Perhaps the Lord will yeeld and pittie vs.
Beare hence theſe wretched blandiſhments of ſinne,
And bring me ſackcloth to attire your King.
Away with pompe, my ſoule is full of woe:
In pittie looke on Niniuie, O God.
                                        Exet. A man.
Alui. Aſſaild with ſhame, with horror ouerborne,
To ſorrowes cold, all guiltie of our ſinne.
Come Ladies come, let vs prepare to pray.
Ah-laſſe, how dare we looke on heauenly light,   2030
That haue diſpilde the maker of the ſame?
How may we hope for mercie from aboue,
That ſtill diſpiſe the warnings from aboue?
Woes me, my conſcience is a heauie foe.
O patron of the poore oppreſt with ſinne,
Looke, looke on me, that now for pittie craue,
Aſſaild with ſhame, with horror ouerborne,
To ſorrow cold, all guiltie of our ſinne.
Come Ladies come, let vs prepare to pray.
                                        Exeunt.   2040
Enter the Vſurer *ſolus*, with a halter in one   *Sc. xvii*
hand, a dagger in the other.

Vſurer. Groning in conſcience, burdened with my crimes,
The hell of ſorrow hauntes me vp and downe.
                                        Tread

Tread where I list, mee-thinkes the bleeding ghostes
Of those whom my corruption brought to noughts,
Do serue for stumbling blocks before my steppes.
The fatherlesse and widow wrongd by me.
The poore oppressed by my vsurie,
Mee-thinkes I see their hands reard vp to heauen,   2050
To crie for vengeance of my couetousnesse.
Where so I walke, Ile sigh and shunne my way.
Thus am I made a monster of the world,
Hell gapes for me, heauen will not hold my soule.
You mountaines shroude me from the God of truth.
Mee-thinkes I see him sit to iudge the earth.
See how he blots me out of the booke of life.
Oh burthen more then Atna that I beare.
Couer me hilles, and shroude me from the Lord.
Swallow me Licas, shield me from the Lord.   2060
In life no peace: each murmuring that I heare,
Mee-thinkes the sentence of damnation soundes,
Die reprobate, and hie thee hence to hell.

> The euill angell tempteth him, offering
> the knife and rope.

What fiend is this that temptes me to the death?
What is my death the harbour of my rest?
Then let me die: what second charge is this?
Mee-things I heare a voice amidst mine eares,
That bids me staie: and tels me that the Lord   2070
Is mercifull to those that do repent.
May I repent? oh thou my doubtfull soule?
Thou maist repent, the Iudge is mercifull.
Hence tooles of wrath, stales of temptation,
For I will pray and sigh vnto the Lord.
In sackcloth will I sigh, and fasting pray:
O Lord in rigor looke not on my sinnes.

> He sits him downe in sack-cloathes, his hands
> and eyes reared to heauen.
>   Enters

Enters Aluida with her Ladies, with difpiearfed lookes.   2080

Alui. Come mournfull dames laie off your b;od;ed locks,
And on your fhoulders fp;ed difpiearfed haires,
Let voice of muficke ceafe, where fo;row dwels.
Cloathed in fackcloaths, figh your finnes with me.
Bemone your p;ide, bewaile your lawleffe lufts,
With fafting mo;tifie your pampered loines:
Oh thinke vpon the ho;rour of your finnes.
Think, think, with me, the burthen of your blames,
Woe to thy pompe, fal,e beautie, fading floure,
Blafted by age, by ficknesse, and by death.   2090
Woe to our painted cheekes, our curious oyles,
Our rich array, that foftered vs in finne.
Woe to our idle thoughts that wound our foules.
Oh would to God all nations might receiue,
A good example by our greeuous fall.

Ladies. You that are planted there where pleafure dwels,
And thinkes your pompe as great as Niniuies,
May fall fo; finne as Niniuie doth now.

Alui. Mourne, mourne, let moane be all your melodie,
And p;ay with me, and I will p;ay fo; all.   2100

Lord. O Lo;d of heauen fo;giue vs our mifdeeds.

Ladies. O Lo;d of heauen fo;giue vs our mifdeeds.

Vfurer. O Lo;d of light fo;giue me my mifdeeds.

*Enters Rafni, the Kings of Affiria, with his nobles
in fackcloath.*

K. Cilicia. Be not fo ouercome with griefe O King,
Leaft you endanger life by fo;rowing fo.

Rafni. King of Cilicia, fhould I ceafe my griefe,
Where as my fwarming finnes afflict my foule?
Vaine man know, this my burthen greater is,   2110
Then euery p;iuate fubiect in my land:
My life hath bene a loadftarre vnto them,
To guide them in the labo;inth of blame,
Thus I haue taught them fo; to do amisse:

Then

Then must I weepe my friend for their amisse,
The fall of Niniuie is wrought by me:
I haue maintaind this Citie in her shame.
I haue contemn'd the warnings from aboue.
I haue vpholden incest, rape, and spoyle.
Tis I that wrought the sinne, must weepe the sinne.   2120
Oh had I teares like to the siluer streames,
That from the Alpine Mountains sweetly streame,
Or had I sighes the treasures of remorse,
As plentifull as Æolus hath blasts,
I then would tempt the heauens with my laments,
And pierce the throane of mercy by my sighes.
    K. Cil. Heauens are prepitious vnto faithful praiers.
    Rasni. But after our repent, we must lament:
Least that a worser mischiefe doth befall.
Oh pray, perhaps the Lord will pitie vs.   2130
Oh God of truth both mercifull and iust,
Behold repentant men with pitious eyes,
We waile the life that we haue led before.
O pardon Lord, O pitie Niniuie.
    Omnes. O pardon Lord, O pitie Niniuie.
    Rasni. Let not the Infants dallying on the tent,
For fathers sinnes in iudgement be opprest.
    K. Cil. Let not the painfull mothers big with childe,
The innocents be punisht for our sinne.
    Rasni. O pardon Lord, O pitie Niniuie.   2140
    Omnes. O pardon Lord, O pitie Niniuie.
    Rasni. O Lord of heauen, the virgins weepe to thee.
The couetous man forie forie for his sinne.
The Prince and poore, all pray before thy throane.
And wilt thou then be wroth with Niniuie ?
    K. Cili. Giue truce to praier O king, and rest a space.
    Rasni. Giue truce to praiers, when times require no truce ?
No Princes no. Let all our subiects hie
Unto our temples, where on humbled knees,
I will exspect some mercy from aboue. Enter the temple Omnes. 2150
                 Enters Ionas, solus.   Sc. xviii
    Ionas. This is the day wherein the Lord hath said
                         I   That

That Niniuie shall quite be ouerthrowne.
This is the day of horror and mishap,
Fatall vnto the curfed Niniuites.
Thefe stately Towers shall in thy watery bounds,
Swift flowing Licas find their burials,
Thefe pallaces the pride of Affurs kings,
Shall be the bowers of defolation,
Where as the follitary bird shall fing,   2160
And Tygers traine their yoong ones to their neft.
O all ye nations bounded by the Weft,
Ye happie Iles where Prophets do abound,
Ye Cities famous in the wefterne world,
Make Niniuie a prefident for you.
Leaue leaud defires, leaue couetous delights.
Flie vfurie, let whoredome be exilde,
Leaft you with Niniuie be ouerthrowne.
Loe how the funnes inflamed torch preuailes,
Scorching the parched furrowes of the earth.   2170
Here will I fit me downe and fire mine eye
Upon the ruines of yon wretched towne,
And lo a pleafant shade, a spreading vine,
To shelter Ionas in this funny heate,
What meanes my God, the day is done and spent.
Lord shall my Prophecie be brought to nought?
When falles the fire? when will the iudge be wroth?
I pray thee Lord remember what I faid,
When I was yet within my country land,
Iehouah is too mercifull I feare.   2180
O let me flie before a Prophet fault,
For thou art mercifull the Lord my God,
Full of compaffion and of fufferance,
And doeft repent in taking punifhment.
Why ftaies thy hand? O Lord firft take my life,
Before my Prophefie be brought to noughts.
Ah he is wroth, behold the gladfome vine
That did defend me from the funny heate,
Is withered quite, and fwallowed by a Serpent.

A Serpent deuoureth the vine. 2190
Now

Now furious Phlegon triumphs on my browes,
And heate preuailes, and I am faint in heart.

Enters the Angell.

Angell. Art thou so angry Ionas? tell me why?

Ionas. Iehouah I with burning heate am plungde,
And shadowed only by a silly vine,
Behold a Serpent hath deuoured it?
And lo the sunne incenst by Easterne winde,
Afflicts me with Cariculer aspect,
Would God that I might die, for well I wot,   2200
Twere better I were dead, then rest aliue.

Angell. Ionas art thou so angry for the vine?

Ionas. Yea I am angry to the death my God.

Angell. Thou hast compassion Ionas on a vine,
On which thou neuer labour didst bestow,
Thou neuer gauest it life or power to grow,
But sodeinly it sprung, and sodeinly dide.
And should not I haue great compassion
On Niniuie the Citie of the world,
Wherein there are a hundred thousand soules,   2210
And twentie thousand infants that ne wot
The right hand from the left, beside much cattle.
Oh Ionas, looke into their Temples now,
And see the true contrition of their King:
The subiects teares, the sinners true remorse.
Then from the Lord proclaime a mercie day,
For he is pitifull as he is iust.

Exet Angelus.

Ionas. I go my God to finish thy command,
Oh who can tell the wonders of my God,   2220
Or talke his praises with a feruent toong.
He bringeth downe to hell, and lifts to heauen.
He drawes the yoake of bondage from the iust,
And lookes vpon the Heathen with pitious eyes:
To him all praise and honour be ascribed.
Oh who can tell the wonders of my God,
He makes the infant to proclaime his truth,

The Aſſe to ſpeake, to ſaue the Prophets life.
The earth and ſea to yeeld increaſe for man.
Who can deſcribe the compaſſe of his power?   2230
Or teſtifie in termes his endleſſe might?
My rauiſht ſpright, oh whither doeſt thou wend?
Go and proclaime the mercy of my God.
Relieue the carefull hearted Niniuites.
And as thou weart the meſſenger of death,
Go bring glad tydings of recouered grace.

Enters Adam ſolus, with a bottle of beere in one ſlop,   Sc. xix
and a great peece of beefe in an other.

Well good-man Ionas, I would you had neuer come from Iury
to this Countrp, you haue made me looke like a leane rib of roaſt 2240
beefe, or like the picture of lent, painted vpon a read-herings cob.
Alaſſe maiſters, we are commanded by the proclamation to faſt
and pray, by my troth I could prettely ſo, ſo, away with praying,
but for faſting, why tis ſo contrary to my nature, that I had rather ſuffer a ſhort hanging, then a long faſting. Marke me, the
words be theſe. Thou ſhalt take no maner of foode for ſo many
daies. I had as leeue he ſhould haue ſaid, thou ſhalt hang thy ſelfe
for ſo many daies. And yet in faith I need not finde fault with the
proclamation, for I haue a buttry, and a pantry, and a kitchen, a-
bout me, for proofe, *Ecce ſignum*, this right ſlop is my pantry, be- 2250
hold a manchet, this place is my kitchin, for loe a peece of beefe.
Oh let me repeat that ſweet word againe: For loe a peece of beef.
This is my buttry, for ſee, ſee, my friends, to my great ioy, a bottle of beere. Thus alaſſe I make ſhift to weare out this faſting,
I driue away the time, but there go Searchers about to ſeeke if
any man breakes the Kings command. Oh here they be, in with
your victuals Adam.

Enters two Searchers.

1. Searcher. How duly the men of Niniuie keep the proclamation, how are they armde to repentance? we haue ſearcht through 2260
the whole Citie & haue not as yet found one that breaks the faſt.

2. Sear. The ſigne of the more grace, but ſtaie, here ſits one
mee-thinkes at his praiers, let vs ſee who it is.

1. Sear. Tis Adam, the Smithes man, how now Adam?

Adam. Trouble me not, thou ſhalt take no maner of foode, but
faſt

fast and pray.

1. Sear. How deuoutly he sits at his orysons, but staie, mee=thinkes I feele a smell of some meate or bread about him.

2. Sear. So thinkes me too, you sirrha, what victuals haue you about you? 2270

Adam. Uictuals! Oh horrible blasphemie! Hinder me not of my praier, nor driue me not into a chollor, victailes! why hardst thou not the sentence, thou shalt take no foode but fast and pray?

2. Sear. Truth so it should be, but me-thinkes I smell meate about thee.

Adam. About me my friends, these words are actions in the Case, about me, No, no: hang those gluttons that cannot fast and pray.

1. Sear. Well, for all your words, we must search you.

Adam. Search me, take heed what you do, my hose are my ca= 2280 stles, tis burglary if you breake ope a slop, no officer must lift vp an iron hatch, take heede my slops are iron.

2. Sear. Oh villaine, see how he hath gotten victailes, bread, beefe, and beere, where the King commanded vpon paine of death none should eate for so many daies, no not the sucking infant.

Adam. Alasse sir, this is nothing but a *modicum non necet vt me-dicus daret,* why sir, a bit to comfort my stomacke.

1. Sear. Uillaine thou shalt be hangd for it.

Adam. These are your words, I shall be hangd for it, but first answer me to this question, how many daies haue we to fast stil? 2290

2. Sear. Fiue daies.

Adam. Fiue daies, a long time, then I must be hangd?

1. Sear. I marry must thou.

Adam. I am your man, I am for you sir, for I had rather be hangd thē abide so long a fast, what fiue daies? come ile vntrusse, is your halter and the gallowes, the ladder, and all such furniture in readinesse?

1. Sear. I warrant thee, shalt want none of these.

Adam. But heare you, must I be hangd?

1. Sear. I marry. 2300

Adam. And for eating of meate, then friends, know ye by these presents, I will eate vp all my meate, and drink vp all my drink, for it shall neuer be said, I was hangd with an emptie stomake.

I   3   1. Sear.

1. Sear. Come away knaue, wilt thou ſtand feeding now?

Adam. If you be ſo haſtie, hang your ſelfe an houre while I come to you, foꝛ ſurely I will eate vp my meate.

2. Sear. Come lets dꝛaw him away perfoꝛce.

Adam. You ſay there is fiue daies yet to faſt, theſe are your

2. Sear. I ſir.   (woꝛds.

Adam. I am foꝛ you, come lets away, and yet let me be put in 2310 the Chꝛonicles.

Enter Ionas, Raſni, Aluida, kings of Cilicia, others royally attended   *Sc. xx*

Ionas. Come carefull King, caſt off thy mournfull weedes,
Exchange thy cloudie lookes to ſmothed ſmiles,
Thy teares haue pierc'd the pitious thꝛoane of grace,
Thy ſighes like Imence pleaſing to the Loꝛd:
Haue bene peace-offerings foꝛ thy foꝛmer pꝛide.
Reioyce and pꝛaiſe his name that gaue thee peace.
And you faire Nymphs, ye louely Niniuites,
Since you haue wept and faſted foꝛ the Loꝛd,   2320
He gratiouſly haue tempered his reuenge,
Beware hencefooꝛth to tempt him any moꝛe,
Let not the niceneſſe of your beautious lookes,
Ingraft in you a high pꝛeſuming minde,
Foꝛ thoſe that climbe, he caſteth to the ground,
And they that humble be, he lifts aloft.

Raſni. Lowly I bend with awfull bent of eye,
Befoꝛe the dꝛead Iehouah, God of hoſte,
Deſpiſing all pꝛophane deuice of man,
Thoſe luſtfull lures that whilome led awɹy,   2330
My wanton eyes ſhall wound my heart no moꝛe:
And the whoſe youth in dalliance I abuſ'd,
Shall now at laſt become my wedlocke mate.
Faire Aluida looke not ſo woe begone:
If foꝛ thy ſinne thy ſoꝛrow do exceed,
Bleſſed be thou, come with a holy band,
Lets knit a knot to ſalue our foꝛmer ſhame.

Alui. With bluſhing lookes betokening my remoꝛſe,
I lowly yeeld my King to thy beheſt,
So as this man of God ſhall thinke it good.   2340

Ionas. Woman, amends may neuer come too late.

                                      The

A will to practice gooduesse, vertuous.
The God of heauen when sinners do repent,
Doth more reioyce then in ten thousand iust.

   Rasni. Then witnesse holie Prophet our accord.

   Alui. Plight in the presence of the Lord thy God.

   Ionas. Blest may you be, like to the flouring sheaues,
That plaie with gentle windes in sommer tide,
Like Oliue branches let your children spred:
And as the Pines in loftie Libanon,   2350
Or as the Kids that feede on Lepher plaines,
So be the seede and offspring of your loines.

       Enters the Vsurer, Gentleman, and Alcon.

   Vsurer. Come foorth my friends whom wittingly I wrongd,
Before this man of God receiue your due,
Before our King I meane to make my peace.
Ionas behold in signe of my remorse,
I heare restore into these poore mens hands,
Their goods which I vniustly haue detaind,
And may the heauens so pardon my misdeeds,   2360
As I am penitent for my offence.

   Thrasi. And what through want from others I purloynd,
Behold O King, I proffer fore thy throane:
To be restord to such as owe the same.

   Ionas. A vertuous deed pleasing to God and man,
Would God all Cities drowned iu like shame,
Would take example of these Niniuites.

   Rasni. Such be the fruites of Niniuies repent,
And such for euer may our dealings be,
That he that cald vs home in height of sinne,   2370
May smile to see our hartie penitence.
Uiceroyes proclaime a fast vnto the Lord,
Let Israels God be honoured in our land.
Let all occasion of corruption die.
For who shall fault therein, shall suffer death.
Beare witnesse God, of my vnfained zeale.
Come holie man, as thou shalt counsaile me,
My Court and Citie shall reformed be.

               Exeunt.

                 Ionas.

Ionas. Wend on in peace, and proſecute this courſe,   2380
You Flanders on whom the milder aire
Doth ſweetly breath the balme of kinde increaſe:
Whoſe lands are fatned with the deaw of heauen,
And made more fruitfull then Actean plaines.
You whom delitious pleaſures dandle ſoft:
Whoſe eyes are blinded with ſecuritie,
Unmaſke your ſelues, caſt error cleane aſide.
O London, mayden of the miſtreſſe Ile,
Wrapt in the foldes and ſwathing cloutes of ſhame:
In thee more ſinnes then Niniuie containes,   2390
Contempt of God, diſpight of reuerend age.
Neglect of law, deſire to wrong the poore:
Corruption, whordome, drunkenneſſe, and pride.
Swolne are thy browes with impudence and ſhame.
O proud adulterous glorie of the Weſt,
Thy neighbors burns, yet doeſt thou feare no fire.
Thy Preachers crie, yet doeſt thou ſtop thine eares.
The larum rings, yet ſleepeſt thou ſecure.
London awake, for feare the Lord do frowne,
I ſet a looking Glaſſe before thine eyes.   2400
O turne, O turne, with weeping to the Lord,
And thinke the praiers and vertues of thy Queene,
Defers the plague which otherwiſe would fall.
Repent O London, leaſt for thine offence,
Thy ſhepheard faile, whom mightie God preſerue,
That ſhe may bide the pillar of his Church,
Againſt the ſtormes of Romiſh Antichriſt:
The hand of mercy ouerſhead her head,
And let all faithfull ſubiects ſay,   Amen.

F I N I S.

B 2 AND B 3 FROM THE EDITION OF 1598

London and England.

Smith. Paltry Smith, why you incarnatiue knaue, what are you, that you speak pettie treason against the Smiths trade?

Clowne. Why flaue, I am a gentleman of Niniuie.

Smith. A Gentleman good sir, I remember you well and al your progenitors, your father bare office in our towne, an honest man he was, and in great discredit in the parish, for they bestow= ed two squires liuings on him, the one was on workingdayes, and then he kept the towne stage, and on holidaies they made him the Sextens man, for he whipt dogs out of the Church. Alas sir, your father, why sir mee-thinks I see the Gentleman stil, a proper youth he was faith, aged some foure & ten, his beard Rats colour, halfe blacke, halfe white, his nose was in the highest de= gree of noses, it was nose Autem glorificam, so set with Rubies, that after his death it should haue bin nailed vp in Copper-smiths hall for a monument. Well sir, I was beholding to your good fa= ther, for he was the first man that euer instructed me in the my= sterie of a pot of Ale.

2. Well said Smith, that crost him ouer the thumbs.

Clowne. Uillaine were it not that we goe to be merrie, my ra= pier should presently quit thy opprobrious termes.

O Peter, Peter, put vp thy sword I prithie heartily into thy scab= bard, hold in your rapier, for though I haue not a long reacher, I haue a short hitter. Nay then gentlemen stay me, for my choller begins to rise against him: for mark the words of a paltry Smith, Oh horrible sentence, thou hast in these words I will stand to it, libelled against all the sound horses, whole horses, sore horses, Coursers, Curtalls, Iades, Cuts, Hacknies, and Mares: where= vpon my friend, in their defence, I giue thee this curse, thou shalt be worth a horse of thine owne this seuen yeare.

1. Clowne. I prithie Smith is your occupation so excellent? A paltry Smith, why ile stand to it, a Smith is Lord of the foure elements, for our iron is made of the earth, our bellowes blowe out aire, our store holdes fire, and our forge water. Nay sir, we reade in the Chronicles, that there was a God of our occupa= tion.

B 2   I

Clowne. J, but he was a Cuckold.

That was the reason sir he cald your father cousin, paltry smith, why in this one word thou hast defaced their worshipful occu= 240 pation.

Clowne. As how?

Marrie sir I will stand to it, that a Smith in his kinde is a Phisition, a Surgion and a Barber. For let a Horse take a cold, or be troubled with the bots, and we straight giue him a potiō or a purgation, in such phisicall maner that he mends straight, if he haue outward diseases, as the spuing, splent, ring-bone, windgall or fashion, or sir a galled back, we let him blood & clap a plaister to him with a pestilence, that mends him with a berie vengeance, now if his mane grow out of order, and he haue 250 any rebellious haires, we straight to our sheeres and trim him with what cut it please vs, pick his eares and make him neat, marry indeed sir, we are slouens for one thing, we neuer vse any musk=balls to wash him with, & the reason is sir, because he can woe without kissing.

Clowne. Well sirrha, leaue off these praises of a Smyth, and bring vs to the best Ale in the towne.

Now sir I haue a feate aboue all the Smyths in Niniuie, for sir, I am a Philosopher that can dispute of the nature of Ale, for marke you sir, a pot of ale consists of foure parts, Imprimis the 260 Ale, the Toast, the Ginger and the Nutmeg.

Clowne. Excellent.

The Ale is a restoratiue, bread is a binder, marke you sir two excellent points in phisicke, the Ginger, oh ware of that: the philosophers haue written of the nature of ginger, tis expulsitiue in two degrees, you shal here the sentēce of Galen, it wil make a man belch, cough, & fart, and is a great comfort to the heart, a proper poesie I promise you, but now to the noble vertue of the Nutmeg, it is saith one Ballad, I think an English Roman was the authour, an vnderlayer to the braines, for when the 270 Ale giues a buffet to the head, oh the Nutmeg that keepes him for a while in temper.

Thus you see the discription of the vertue of a pot of Ale, now sir

to

to put my phisicall precepts in practise follow me, but afoze I step
any further.

Clowne. Whats the matter now?

Why seeing I haue prouided the Ale, who is the puruaioz foz the
wenches, foz maisters take this of me, a cup of Ale without a
wench, why alasse tis like an egge without salt, oz a red hering
without musterd.   280

Lead vs to the Ale, weele haue wenches inough I warrant thee.

Oseas. Iniquitie seekes out companions still,
And mortall men are armed to do ill:
London looke on, this matter nips thee neere,
Leaue off thy ryot, pride and sumptuous cheere.
Spend lesse at boord, and spare not at the doore,
But aid the infant, and releeue the poore.
Else seeking mercy, being mercilesse,
Thou be adiudged to endlesse heauinesse.

      Enters the Vsurer, a yoong Gentleman, and   *Sc. iv*
                   a poore man.   291

Vsurer. Come on, I am euery day troubled with those needie
companions, what newes with you, what wind bzings you hi=
ther?

Gent. Sir I hope how far soeuer you make it off, you remem=
ber too well foz me, that this is the day wherein I should pay you
money that I tooke vp of you alate in a commoditie.

Poore man. And sir, sirreuerence of your manhood and gente=
rie, I haue bzought home such mony as you lent me.

Vsurer. You yoong Gentleman, is my mony readie?   300

Gentle. Trulie sir, this time was so shozt, the commoditie so
bad, and the pzomise of friends so bzoken, that I could not pzouide
it against the day, wherefoze I am come to intreat you to stand
my friend, and to fauour me with a longer time, and I will make
you sufficient consideration.

Vsurer. Is the winde in that dooze, if thou hast my mony so it
is, I will not defer a day, an houre, a minute, but take the fozfeyt

of the bond.

Gent. I pray you ſir conſider that my loſſe was great by the commoditie I tooke vp, you knowe ſir I borrowed of you forty pounds, whereof I had ten ponnds in money, and thirtie pounds in Lute ſtrings, which when I came to ſell againe, I could get but fiue pounds for them, ſo had I ſir but fifteene pounds for my fortie: In conſideration of this ill bargaine, I pray yon ſir giue me a month longer. [310]

Vſurer. I anſwered thee afore not a minute, what haue I to do how thy bargain prooued, I haue thy hand ſet to my book, that thou receiuedſt fortie pounds of me in money.

Gent. I ſir it was your deuice that, to colour the Statute, but your conſcience knowes what I had. [320]

Poore. Freend, thou ſpeakeſt hebrew to him, when thou tal= keſt to him of conſcience, for he hath as much conſcience about the forfeyt of an Obligation, as my blind Mare God bleſſe her, hath ouer a manger of Oates.

Gent. Then there is no fauour ſir?

Vſurer. Come to morrow to mee, and ſee how I will vſe thee.

Gent. No couetous Caterpiller, know, that I haue made ex= treame ſhift rather then I would fall into the hands of ſuch a ra= uening panthar: and therefore here is thy mony and deliuer me the recogniſance of my lands. [330]

Vſurer. What a ſpite is this, hath ſped of his Crownes, if he had miſt but one halfe houre, what a goodly Farme had I got= ten for fortie pounds, well tis my curſed fortune. Oh haue I no ſhift to make him forfeit his recogniſance.

Cent. Come ſir will you diſpatch and tell your mony?

Strikes 4. a clocke.

Vſurer. Stay, what is this a clocke foure, let me ſee, to be paid between the houres of three and foure in the afternoone, this goes right for me: you ſir, heare you not the clocke, and haue you not a counterpaine of your Obligation? the houre is paſt, it was to bee paid betweene three and foure, and now the clocke hath ſtrooken foure, [340]

LIST OF IRREGULAR AND DOUBTFUL READINGS
(1598, B 2 AND B 3)

222 oppropitous
230–1 fhalt | be
281 weele (final e broken and doubtful)
306 hall my
311 ponnds
314 pon
334 fortune. (period doubtful)
336 Cent.
338 Vfurer. (*first* r *doubtful*)
341 counterpaine

The speaker's name seems to be omitted before lines 223, 233, 239, 243, 258, 263, 277, and 281. The new paragraph at 273 is anomalous.